Thomas Pelham-Holles Newcastle

A narrative of the changes in the ministry

1765-1767

Thomas Pelham-Holles Newcastle

A narrative of the changes in the ministry
1765-1767

ISBN/EAN: 9783337113315

Printed in Europe, USA, Canada, Australia, Japan

Cover: Foto ©ninafisch / pixelio.de

More available books at **www.hansebooks.com**

CHANGES IN THE MINISTRY

1765—1767

A NARRATIVE

OF THE

CHANGES IN THE MINISTRY

1765—1767

TOLD BY THE DUKE OF NEWCASTLE
IN A SERIES OF LETTERS TO JOHN WHITE, M.P.

EDITED FOR THE ROYAL HISTORICAL SOCIETY
BY
MARY BATESON

LONGMANS, GREEN, AND CO.
39 PATERNOSTER ROW, LONDON
NEW YORK AND BOMBAY
1898

PREFACE

THE writing of Narratives or Memorials of political negotiations was a favourite exercise with eighteenth-century statesmen; it was a method of self-expression which could not fail to commend itself to Thomas Pelham-Holles, Duke of Newcastle (1693-1768). He was a man to whom a confidant was indispensable, to whom correspondence was the salt of life. While Lord Hardwicke lived, it was to him that he most often disburdened himself of his complaints, grievances, and views; on his death, in 1764, his place was taken by the Duke's old friend, John White of Walling Wells, M.P. for East Retford 1733-1768. Walpole describes him as an old republican who governed both the Duke of Newcastle and Lord John Cavendish,[1] and his interest with the Cavendishes is frequently alluded to in the present Narrative. One of his chief claims to fame is that Burke originally purposed to dedicate to him his 'Thoughts on the Present Discontents,'[2] and it is known that he became the recipient of many ministerial confidences.[3] Towards the close of his life, the Duke of New-

---

[1] *George III.* ed. Barker, ii. 106.
[2] Burke's *Correspondence*, i, 182. Macknight's *Burke*, i. 393.
[3] Albemarle's *Rockingham*, ii. 20, note: 'The heads of the party admitted him to their secret conciliabula.'

castle addressed to him the following series of letters, which he intended to serve as a narrative of the political intrigues in which he was concerned 1765-7, and the collection now forms one volume of the Newcastle Correspondence, Add. MSS. 33003. Although the Narrative is headed 'very secret,' from the care that has been taken in making duplicates[1] in enriching it with marginal notes and an appendix of illustrative matter[2] it would seem not impossible that the Duke intended it for ultimate publication.

The Narrative covers the period of continual ministerial changes which followed on the dismissal of George Grenville and preceded the rise of Lord North, the period in which it was generally believed by the Whigs that Lord Bute ruled the King's counsels. Secretaries of State and Lords of the Treasury were rapidly shifting; 'surely you did not think,' says Walpole satirically, that they 'are of more importance or ought to be more permanent than churchwardens?' It is with the rise and fall of the Rockingham Ministry and with the unsuccessful negotiation for a coalition, which followed on the failure of Lord Chatham's health, that the Duke's Narrative is principally concerned.

The first letter opens with an account of the attempts of George III. to get rid of the obnoxious Bedford-Grenville Ministry by means of a negotiation which should create a Ministry from some section of the Whig Opposition. To arrange terms with either the Duke of Newcastle and the younger members of the party, or with Pitt and Temple, the King engaged the services of his uncle, the Duke of Cumberland, who himself wrote a Memorial of these events. The Duke of Cumberland's dislike of Lord Bute had hitherto

---

[1] Only a small portion is extant in the Duke's own hand. The copy seems to be in the hand of his chaplain, Dr. Thomas Hurdis.

[2] This no longer forms part of the volume, and appears to be lost.

kept him out of the King's favour, but as it was now obvious that, with whichever party the King negotiated, terms more or less exacting on the subject of Lord Bute and his friends and relations would be made, the differences of uncle and nephew were now overcome. The Duke of Cumberland's Memorial is in the main substantiated by the present Narrative; both statements show that the exclusion of the Princess Dowager from the Regency Bill was early made one of the Duke of Cumberland's requests. The necessity of conceding this point, if the negotiation was to proceed, may explain the King's agreement to Lord Halifax's motion, which was framed to omit his mother. It is more likely that he sacrificed his wishes on that question in the hope of securing a new Ministry than out of dread of the old.

The account that follows serves to explain with clearness the causes of the Duke of Cumberland's first failure to make terms with Pitt and Lord Temple. The main reason of his want of success was Lord Temple's suspicion of Lord Bute's influence, for a report of a plan to give the headship of the Treasury to Lord Northumberland, whose son had married Bute's daughter, had reached Temple's ears, and was in truth sufficiently alarming. Already, too, he was sensible of certain famous 'delicacies,'[1] although he stated expressly that his reconciliation with his brother, George Grenville, did not lay him under any obligation or restraint with regard to public behaviour. Already, too, it was made known that Mr. Pitt, as Lord Temple's brother-in-law, 'might have his delicacies also.' At the time of the Duke of Cumberland's second negotiation

---

[1] See Walpole (ed. Barker), ii. 133: 'But surely Lord Temple was not so overrun with delicacy that he could afford to make a secret of the only delicacy he seems ever to have felt, the turning out his own brother to take his place himself.'

in the following month, when there was no further doubt of the genuineness and directness of the King's offer, these 'delicacies' had become more decided. Pitt was still affirming that he was 'penetrated with His Majesty's goodness, ready, proud and in duty bound to fling himself at His Majesty's feet,' and, according to the Duke of Newcastle, was even persuaded into actual acceptance on being satisfied that the King was 'not averse' to the treaty he proposed with Russia and Prussia. Ultimately, however, Lord Temple's private reasons for refusal necessitated Pitt's withdrawal, as without Lord Temple he felt that he would have no one he could trust to convey his thoughts to His Majesty.

The King was determined not to submit again to the humiliation of a return to the Grenville Ministry, and out of what remained of the Opposition he formed the Rockingham Ministry, which took office July 1765, after some seven weeks of 'administrative anarchy.' The Duke of Newcastle became Privy Seal, and (as he says) at the King's desire he undertook the duty of recommending to all Church preferments. He had hoped that his age and experience might give him a principal sway in the counsels of ministers so young and inexperienced as the Marquis of Rockingham and the Duke of Grafton: but a bitter disillusioning awaited him, and to John White he turns, crying out against their ingratitude.

Although he had taken the Privy Seal 'to be free from the trouble, fatigue, and responsibility of a Minister,' he had fully expected 'to be consulted on every material step in Government either with regard to measures or men'—men particularly. Walpole writes of him at this time as 'busy in restoring clerks and tide-waiters, in offering everybody everything, and in patronising the clergy again ; not being yet cured by their behaviour of loving to make bishops.' Yet he was not half so busy as he wished to be. He was, however, a great deal more busy than Pitt wished him to be.

Early in December 1765 he was urging, as others were urging, the necessity of an application to Pitt, whose services in foreign affairs appeared to him to be 'more wanted than ever.' He did not then know that it was his own presence in the Ministry that was a main obstacle in the way of Pitt's adherence. In the summer Pitt had written to a friend : 'Claremont could not be to me an object of confidence or expectation of a solid system for the public good, according to my notions of it,' and in December he had come to the conclusion that the Duke's eagerness for his help was 'nothing but a little artifice to hold out to the public an appearance of connection where he knows he has none, and I know he never shall have any.' 'When his Grace does me the honour to say that anything is exactly conformable to *my ideas*, he is pleased to use the name of a man who has never communicated his ideas to the Duke of Newcastle upon the present state of affairs, and who is finally resolved never to be in confidence or concert again with his Grace.' 'I have been so often sacrificed' by the Duke of Newcastle, 'I shall never accede to his Grace's Ministry.' It has been thought that Pitt was unnecessarily fearful of Newcastle's influence, and on this question the Duke's Narrative throws some light. Although it is full of complaints that his old influence has waned and is waning, it is clear that it was still necessary to reckon with it.

By January 3, 1766, the Duke knew that Pitt made his exclusion a condition, though it would appear that he was not yet aware of the depth of his distrust. In any case, the Duke perceived the futility of resistance, if the Duke of Grafton and Mr. Conway should persist in advising the King to send for

Pitt, and on January 9 he wrote to Lord Rockingham a dignified letter expressing his determination 'to be in no degree himself an obstacle.'[1] Pitt continued to make public allusion to 'that influence which was most suspected,' which was interpreted to be the Duke of Newcastle's,[2] and at length the news reached his Grace that Pitt had refused to sit at Council with him. For a while the Duke sought to adhere to his former position, but in the face of the King's unwillingness to negotiate with Pitt, it was unnecessary for him to offer himself as an immediate sacrifice, and as time went on the wound rankled.

Pitt's real difficulty, it would seem, lay with the King, whose alarm at Pitt's firmness on the American question, fear of finding his advances once more rebuffed through the influence of Lord Temple, and hope that a fairly placable Ministry might stem the tide of popular opinion yet a little longer, all combined to keep him still friendly with the old Duke of Newcastle, whom he always trusted, and unwilling to approach the dangerous Pitt. After Pitt's great speech on the Repeal of the Stamp Act, January 14, the King definitely declined to authorise the Duke of Grafton to approach him.

For a brief space the King hoped to evade the direct issue of the repeal or enforcement of the Stamp Act by a vote for 'modification.' In this the royal influence failed, and Lord Rockingham enjoyed a short-lived triumph over the vote for the repeal. This question settled, a chief difficulty in the way of Pitt's inclusion was removed, and by the end of April the Duke of Grafton made known his intention to resign, in the hope of precipitating a crisis which should force Pitt's return. His resignation failed of the desired effect, for two further difficulties

---

[1] Albemarle's *Rockingham*, i. 265.
[2] *Letters of Charlemont to Flood*, p. 5.

remained, in the King's unwillingness to make advances before he was certain of a successful result, and in his belief that the Duke of Newcastle's activity and experience were fair counterparts for Pitt's genius and judgment. Only the immediate difficulty in filling the Duke of Grafton's place as Secretary of State presented itself. The old Duke nursed a half-hope that he might be pressed to take the office himself, and the King sympathised, it would seem, with the Duke's annoyance when told that Lord Rockingham had been perfectly silent on hearing the suggestion. The appointment of the Duke of Richmond proved merely a temporary expedient for prolonging the Ministry's lingering existence, for it had no real strength of any kind.

Although Lord Rockingham had triumphed in securing the repeal of the Stamp Act, the credit was all Pitt's, and he found himself unable to secure his own way with the King, whenever they differed on any point. By the end of the session the King came to see that Pitt's idea of a Ministry of the ablest men of all parties was one in which he had always believed; and Lord Northington, getting wind of the King's readiness to approach Pitt, made his own resignation of the Chancellorship the signal for a storm which should land him safely in the coming Ministry. The result of his negotiation was that the Duke of Grafton became First Minister, with Pitt, now raised to the peerage, as Privy Seal. Pitt's determination to take this office was bitterly resented by the unhappy Duke of Newcastle, who was called on to resign it. Henceforth he persistently describes himself as 'the first sacrifice to Lord Chatham's boundless ambition.' To the last he cherished the hope that the King would ask him to remain and take office in the Grafton-Chatham Ministry, but he is careful to add that no consideration on earth would have made him accept it. It is not inconceivable, however, that, had the offer been made, his services would have been retained. His sense of party duty was such that he was led to regard the retention of office under most circumstances as dignified rather than contemptible. He praises greatly the conduct of the Duke of Portland, who 'out of generosity and a noble way of thinking,' as he calls it, resisted his inclinations by keeping his employment 'for the sake of the public and the Whig cause,' because resignations would have 'thrown the Earl of Chatham into those hands from whom every violence and destruction to the Whig cause was to be expected.'

The Narrative gives no record of events from August 4, 1766, to July 1767. Walpole writes of the Duke in the summer of 1766 as moving heaven and earth to raise dissatisfaction, 'but heaven and earth are not easily moved with a numbed finger of 70.' Soon, however, the weakness of the Grafton Ministry was to afford him one last opportunity. He writes in July 1767 of the Ministry's growing difficulties, of the total neglect of foreign affairs; the Duke has heard such an account of France as must make every good Englishman tremble, 'their army complete to a man, well-officered, well-appointed, well-paid, their trade flourishing everywhere, and encroaching upon ours.' The weakness and disunion of the Ministry, and Lord Chatham's continued ill-health, led the Duke of Grafton to seek support from the Rockingham party, and to attempt through them a negotiation with the Bedford party. The Duke of Newcastle, though greatly vexed to hear no offer of his own restoration to office, thought he saw his way to act as mediator in this difficult and delicate negotiation, by which he hoped to crown his closing years with success. His efforts to persuade Lord Rockingham to let nothing stand in the way of coalition were unwearying, but naturally enough unavailing, for Lord Rockingham's determination to retain Conway as leader of the House of Commons, and the Duke of Bedford's desire for the inclusion of Grenville, were obviously irreconcilable. Yet the Duke thought that 'the Grenvilles ought to be included at any rate, provided they would yield the Treasury and American department.' 'Conway, learning that the Duke was strongly for George Grenville, would not be commonly civil to him,' but the Duke was blind even to this indication that the personal and party hostilities, which divided factions, so long bitterly opposed, were not likely to be all at once even superficially reconciled. He was certain of the possibility of a lasting reconciliation only because he was eager for it, being weary of 'those Bute fluctuating administrations,' and 'desirous of seeing such a one established as one might support with honour.' The whole negotiation was obviously foredoomed to failure, and with its collapse and a final upbraiding of John White and the Duke of Portland, to whom the whole Narrative was submitted, the Duke of Newcastle's journal abruptly closes.

It cannot be urged that in this singularly naïve piece of self-justification the Duke represents himself as other than he was known to be. The almost unanimous verdict passed upon him by his contemporaries was that 'he was the most capital simpleton that ever the caprice of fortune placed in the high offices which he filled,'[1] and the Narrative may serve to warrant it. That he should have attained a great political position and kept it for some fifty years is one of the surprises of eighteenth-century history; the Narrative will not explain the secret of his power. It is lucid, if ungrammatical, for his natural

[1] See the letter of Selwyn in the Howard MSS., *Fifteenth Report of the Historical MSS. Commission*, p. 230.

simplicity made him incapable of literary obscurity; it is honest, if undignified; it is as self-revealing as the Diary of Pepys, but that it is totally devoid of wisdom is not to be denied. It seems, however, to deserve publication, that it may be used in conjunction with such contemporary narratives as the Duke of Cumberland's 'Memorial,' the Duke of Bedford's 'Private Journal,' Charles Yorke's 'Journal,' and Grenville's 'Diary of Memorable Transactions.'

The capitals and punctuation of the apograph have not been strictly adhered to.

MARY BATESON.

A NARRATIVE

OF THE

CHANGES IN THE MINISTRY, 1765-7

I

Fo. 1. Add. MSS. 33003.   Claremont:[1] June 4, 1765.

SIR,—I am sure you must be desirous to hear the particulars of the rise, progress, and, at last, the miscarriage of the most extraordinary transaction, that ever happen'd in this, or in any other country.

An extraordinary transaction indeed! when an opportunity offer'd, which no one man could ever hope for; that the removal of an administration, which, by their conduct, had render'd themselves so disagreeable to the nation, should be proposed by the King, and not take effect! the removal of which administration had been the avowed principle, and view, of all those, *united*, which were called the *Opposition*; which had made so many formidable but yet unsuccessful attempts, in both Houses, for that purpose; and which Opposition, from desertions, varieties of opinion, and varieties of views amongst themselves, and by the unjustifiable acts of power and influence of the Crown, had been so reduced, that any attempt, in either House, upon any the most

---

[1] The house at Esher, not the present building.

urgent, and most justifiable occasion was scarcely ventured upon ; and every body had given over *almost* the thoughts of Opposition to the administration. In these circumstances, the Crown itself, —sensible of the inability of the present Ministers and of the ill consequences of their remaining in their offices—flings itself, as it were, into the Opposition, to form an administration amongst themselves, which the King was desirous to take ; and would undoubtedly have supported : so that without being liable to the trite, common objections of *forcing the Crown,—coming in without the King's approbation,—being not sure of the King's support*, &c., His Majesty was the first proposer ;—wanted only to get rid of his *present* obnoxious Ministers ; and settle such an administration as might be agreeable to the Nation, and particularly to the true friends of his family, the Whigs. And, to evince all the world of this truth, was pleased to make use of the most proper person, His Royal Highness the Duke of Cumberland, (in whom all true friends of the Government had, or ought to have the greatest confidence,) to bring it about ; and yet, that this should miscarry, and the Ministers remain in their places! I call an extraordinary event.

I shall now give you as exact an account, as my memory can serve me with, of the several particulars, which have come to my knowledge, which have passed in this negotiation ; and I believe, the Duke, or my Lord Albemarle, have told me every thing, that was material.[1]

---

[1] The Duke of Cumberland drew up a Memorial on his negotiation, April to May, which is published in Albemarle's *Memoirs of the Marquis of Rockingham*, i. 185. The dates of the earlier part (to p. 190) are substantiated by the Duke of Newcastle's account. From p. 191 onwards the Duke of Cumberland has antedated events by a week. The mistake seems to have arisen from a confusion between the dates of the first passing of the Regency Bill in the House of Lords and the second passing, after it had been amended by the House of Commons. Cf. *Grenville Correspondence*, iii. 175 *note* ; 224 *note*. Also, for accounts of the negotiation and the Regency Bill Debate see Charles Yorke's Journal in Harris's *Hardwicke*, iii. 445, and Phillimore's *Lyttelton*, ii. 664. And, for the Duke of Cumberland's negotiation, Almon's *Anecdotes of Eminent Persons*, ii. 41 *sqq.*, and *Anecdotes of the Earl of Chatham*, i. 465 *sqq.*

On Monday morning, the 15th of April, (the last time His Royal Highness came from Newmarket,) he order'd me to attend him, at Cumberland House; and then gave me an account of what had passed with the King,—the Sunday that His Royal Highness went to Newmarket,[1] and with my Lord Northumberland—afterwards at Newmarket.

N.B.—Great part of my Lord Northumberland's conversation was with my Lord Albemarle.

His Royal Highness had received a message from the King to attend His Majesty, that—Sunday morning, at nine o'clock, before he went to Newmarket; which the Duke did accordingly

His Majesty was extremely gracious to His Royal Highness; and began by saying, that as he had been ill, thank God he was then quite recovered, he had been thinking what confusion this country would be in, if an accident should happen to him, whilst his children were under age; that, for that reason, he was determined to have a Regency settled immediately; that this was his own thoughts, and not any of his Ministers'; that he had talked separately upon it to his four Ministers, viz. the Duke of Bedford, Mr. Grenville, and the two Secretaries of State; and that he had order'd them to consider in what manner it was to be done; but that His Majesty wanted His Royal Highness's opinion and advice; as nobody knew better what to do, than the Duke did. And, I think, something as if His Royal Highness might have something to do in it.

The Duke of Cumberland then represented to His Majesty, that (God be prais'd!) His Majesty's health was now so good that there did not seem to be the least occasion for any hurry; that this was a question that required very mature consideration; that it was then the month of April; and there did not seem to be time enough, this Session, for such a thorough consideration, as an affair of this importance required. And I am not sure that His Royal Highness did not touch, at a distance, upon the

[1] April 7.

difficult part of the question [1]; upon which, however, His Royal Highness explained himself fully in the course of the transaction.

The King answer'd very peremptorily,—that it was his own thought, and that it must be carried into execution *this Session*.

His Majesty also, to the best of my remembrance, let drop some dissatisfaction with his present Ministers; and the Duke of Cumberland made some very short reply, lamenting that the old and true friends of His Majesty's Royal Family and Government were excluded from his service. To which His Majesty replied that it was not his fault; he proscribed nobody; or to that effect.[2]

At Newmarket, my Lord Northumberland had had two conferences with the Duke of Cumberland; which, tho' His Royal Highness did not know it then, his Lordship declared afterwards, to have been by His Majesty's order.

In these conferences, my Lord Northumberland explained very fully His Majesty's dissatisfaction with his present Ministers; and, that he was determined to part with them: and to my Lord Albemarle he said, the King was determined to fling himself into the Duke's hands.

His Lordship, however, insisted with the Duke, that the affair of the Regency could not be postponed; that that must be immediately settled.

The Duke represented most strongly against it; and particularly, the strange appearance it would have, to let these Ministers have the conduct of such a material measure as this, and to turn them out, immediately after; when it had not been possible for them, to have given any new offence.

And I believe, His Royal Highness explain'd himself then, or soon after, upon the difficulty there would be, if the Princess Dowager of Wales should be amongst those, who should be

[1] The Princess Dowager's position.
[2] On the King's recent treatment of the Duke of Cumberland see *Lecky*, iii. 90.

qualified by this Act of Parliament to be Regent of these Kingdoms.

To that, I think, it was, soon after, answer'd, that the Bill should be so framed, that that should not be practicable[1]; for that none were properly of the King's Family but the descendants of His Majesty's ancestors; and, that that would appear plainly by the Bill; for that the Queen should be named, by name, as one capable; which Her Majesty need not be, if she was of the King's Family, and would then be capable, by the general clause.

There was also, I think, at Newmarket, or I am sure, in all the conferences afterwards with my Lord Northumberland, a good deal of discourse about my Lord Bute; which varied, on the part of my Lord Northumberland, almost at every meeting.

At first, that my Ld. Bute was not to have any employment; that he was sensible how wrong it would be; and also, the prejudice, which his being in the stations he had been in, had been to His Majesty's affairs. And once, the Duke of Cumberland had my Lord Bute's thanks, by my Lord Northumberland, for having, by what had passed, induced the King to consent, that my Lord Bute should have no employment.

At other times, the contrary was as much press'd; that the King would have my Lord Bute have some employment, tho' not ministerial; and once, it was proposed, that his Lordship should have some Cabinet Council office, upon a previous assurance, that he should never be summon'd to the Cabinet Council.

To cut this affair short, the Duke of Cumberland finding that the Regency would not be settled entirely to his satisfaction; that the Bill was brought in in a different way;[2] and that

[1] If this was so, it would explain the King's share in Lord Halifax's amendment (see below), the true nature of which is somewhat obscure. The Duke of Cumberland's Memorial (p. 190) also serves to show that the negotiation with the Opposition affected the terms of the Regency Bill.

[2] Leaving the question of the inclusion of the Princess Dowager open.

there was still a hankering after my Lord Bute's having an office, which could not be admitted, His Royal Highness told my Lord Northumberland, that he look'd upon the negotiation as broke, and over.

My Lord Northumberland said, *he hoped not*: but in such a manner, as His Royal Highness did not imagine, that he should ever hear any more of it; and, I believe, the Duke was confirmed in that opinion, by having never had an order to attend the King, tho' my Lord Northumberland frequently talked of it.

I should have observ'd, that, from the beginning, His Royal Highness was determined to ask the King's leave to communicate the whole to Mr. Pitt, the moment that there should appear to be any thing serious in it; and to propose that Mr. Pitt should be the principal part of the new administration to be formed. And indeed, His Royal Highness told me, the first time he did me the honour to mention this affair to me, on Monday, the 15th of April, that he intended immediately to ask leave to communicate it to Mr. Pitt.

My Lord Northumberland threw out early, (I think at Newmarket,) that it was proposed, that he himself, if approved, should be at the head of the Treasury, with Lord Barrington, or Lord North, Chancellor of the Exchequer.[1]

My Lord Northumberland saw the Duke several times after his return to town. Nothing material passed; the same supposed resolution in His Majesty, to part with his present Ministers; some loose conversations about employments; Mr. Pitt, to be Secretary of State, I think, with Charles Townshend; Lord Temple, some high office; the Duke of Newcastle, to be President of the Council[2]; and, I think, the Marquess of Rockingham, Lord Chamberlain.

The Duke of Cumberland assured His Lordship that the Duke of Newcastle would not take President of the Council, or

---

[1] These wild suggestions are known only from this source.
[2] Cf. Albemarle's *Rockingham*, i. 195.

any office whatever but the Privy Seal; and why should not he be Privy Seal?

To which Lord Northumberland replied, that as His Majesty had a regard for my experience, the King wished to have the Duke of Newcastle of the *Conciliabulum*,[1] where all business of consequence was first settled; which the Privy Seal was not, (the Privy Seal perhaps reserved for another person.)

The moment the Duke told me this, I assured His Royal Highness, that no consideration should make me accept the President; or any office, but that of Privy Seal, which could not be called a ministerial one.

But afterwards in discourse with my Lord Lyttelton, and upon His Lordship's telling me, a Lord Privy Seal might *be Minister*, I replied, why then I will not take it; *let them give it to the Duke of Portland*; and it will please me as well, or better.

But, as I said before, from what passed in these visits upon the point of the Regency, and the constant change of conversation about Lord Bute's having an employment, or not, the Duke thought, that there was an end of the whole, and that this negotiation was quite broke off.

As the transaction about the Regency Bill was probably one of the greatest causes, or, at least, was the most publick indication of an open disagreement between my Lord Bute, and the Ministers, viz. Duke of Bedford, Mr. Grenville, &c., I shall give the best account I can of that transaction.

There had certainly been differences of opinion, whether the Princess Dowager of Wales should be excluded absolutely, or that be left to the doubtful interpretation, whether Her Royal Highness could properly be said *to be of the King's Royal Family*, or *not*.

It was pretended that as the Queen was particularly named, it was clear from thence, that the Queen would not have been included, if Her Majesty had not been particularly named, and

[1] 'That silly term,' the Duke calls it in a letter of March 13, 1757.

consequently, that the Queen would not have been interpreted to be of *the King's Royal Family.*

We argued for the necessity that there should be no doubt upon an affair of such importance; and the Duke of Portland and I were the only Lords, who spoke on that occasion, and were of opinion, that the Queen should be named *Regent* in the Bill. I had put down some words, (the same which Lord Halifax moved a few days after,) confining it to the descendants of the late King. I shew'd these words to the Duke of Bedford. His Grace told me, if it was not clear enough already, that the Princess Dowager would not be qualified by the general clause, confining it to the King's Royal Family, my words would be very proper.

My Lord Chancellor gave his opinion, that the Princess Dowager of Wales, His Majesty's mother, was of the King's Royal Family. That, or some other reason, was the cause that the day after, my Lord Halifax proposed the very words I had shew'd to the Duke of Bedford; and Lord Halifax insinuated, he did it by the King's order, or with His Majesty's consent.[1]

This amendment passed unanimously in the House of Lords:[2] but those who were concerned that Her Royal Highness should not be excluded, prevailed upon Mr. Moreton,[3] to make a motion in the House of Commons for admitting Her Royal Highness the Princess Dowager; which motion was objected to by very few in the House of Commons, and came up to the House of Lords.[4] And—which was very surprizing, the

---

[1] Cf. *Grenville Correspondence*, iii. 150 *sqq.*; Walpole, *Memoirs of George III.*, ed. G. F. R. Barker, ii. 88; Walpole, *Letters*, iv. 350. The Duke of Richmond had proposed that the persons capable of the Regency should be the Queen, the Princess Dowager, and all the descendants of the late King usually resident in England. Lord Halifax's amendment was in the same terms, but omitted the Princess Dowager.

[2] Friday, May 3. See *Grenville Correspondence*, iii. 224.

[3] On John Morton see *Walpole* (Barker), ii. 102 *note*.

[4] *Grenville Correspondence*, iii. 29, 33.

Duke of Bedford and my Lord Halifax himself, who proposed the amendment, submitted, without saying one word to the motion made in the House of Commons, for inserting the name of Her Royal Highness the Princess Dowager, and there was no opposition given to it, in the House of Lords, but by the Duke of Portland and myself.[1]

Soon after this [2] arose the tumults and insurrections of the weavers against the Duke of Bedford. The behaviour of my Lord Bute,[3] and his friends, upon that occasion, greatly irritated the Duke of Bedford and his Party, and was undoubtedly one great cause of what happen'd afterwards.

To His Royal Highness's great surprize, the very night that the Regency Bill (the different appearances,[4] upon that occasion, in the two Houses, I do not mention,) passed the House of Lords, (which I take to have been, Tuesday the 14th day of May,[5]) my Lord Northumberland very unexpectedly came again to His Royal Highness.

The Duke of Cumberland would not suppose he came upon business, and therefore talked of nothing but Newmarket, till Lord Northumberland interrupted him, and would resume the discourse of the negotiation.

His Royal Highness said he looked upon that, as quite over. Lord Northumberland replied, *quite otherwise* ; that the King was determined to part with these Ministers.

The Duke of Cumberland had desired that he might communicate the whole to Mr. Pitt, my Lord Temple, the Duke of Newcastle, and the Marquess of Rockingham. Lord Northumberland replied, the sooner the better. Upon which, His Royal Highness sent my Lord Albemarle to Hayes, and wrote

---

[1] See *Walpole* (Barker), ii. 109, for their speeches.
[2] The tumults came to a crisis on May 15. On the riots see *Bedford Correspondence*, iii. 279 and *note*, and *Walpole* (Barker), ii. 111 *sqq*.
[3] See the Duchess of Bedford's remarks, *Walpole* (Barker), ii. 113.
[4] In the sense probably of 'attendances.' See *N.E.D.*
[5] For Monday, May 13. Cf. *Grenville Correspondence*, iii. 224.

to Stowe to my Lord Temple, to desire he would come to town. Lord Northumberland, I think, dropt that night that there would be no difficulty about Mr. Pitt.

And the next day, about five in the afternoon, Lord Northumberland came to my Lord Albemarle, and told him, that the King desired to see the Duke of Cumberland, that evening, at Richmond; and that His Royal Highness would go from thence to Mr. Pitt at Hayes, that the King would agree to every thing, and to whatever His Royal Highness should propose for Mr. Pitt, and would give His Royal Highness full powers.

The Duke of Cumberland went, that evening, to Richmond; but, as His Royal Highness did not return to town, till near twelve o'clock at night, he was obliged to postpone his journey to Hayes, till the next morning; and he appointed my Lord Temple to meet him at Hayes, which he did.

After His Royal Highness had been some time alone with Mr. Pitt, my Lord Temple and my Lord Albemarle were called in. The conference lasted five hours.

To begin, first, with what passed, at Richmond, with the King and His Royal Highness; which, as well as I can remember the account which was given me of it, was:—

That His Majesty was most extremely gracious to His Royal Highness; expressed the greatest regard for and confidence in him; and shew'd very plainly, that His Majesty was determined to form this new administration by the Duke's advice.

The King declared his uneasiness with his present Ministers, and the causes of it; that they treated him personally ill; that they forced him to do every thing they would, and some things His Majesty did not like; that reversions, pensions, &c. to support themselves, were all they had in view;[1] that they promised *the King* to do great things for the publick, but that His

[1] On the charge of rapacity made against Grenville, see *Walpole* (Barker), ii. 145 note.

Majesty found nothing done; North America greatly discontented, and no proper disposition, or at least no satisfactory one, made of the new acquisitions there; the same discontent at home also. I think, some insinuations, that the credit still remained low, and no great matter done towards the payment of the debt.

But His Majesty insisted strongly upon the personal ill usage of him; that they continually threaten'd His Majesty to quit his service upon the least difficulty which the King made upon any proposal they made to him. The King seem'd most offended with Mr. Grenville, and, after him, with the Duke of Bedford.

His Majesty seem'd to leave the particular adjustment of employments to future consideration; except, (as I understood it,) that Mr. Pitt was to be Secretary of State, and my Lord Temple, at the head of the Treasury; His Majesty saying, that he was sensible, that my Lord Northumberland, (then Lieutenant, as my Lord Temple had called him,[1]) would not do. The King desired the Duke to see Mr. Pitt immediately, and my Lord Temple together, that every thing might be settled.

And, as His Royal Highness had been pleased to order my Lord Rockingham, and myself, to attend him, that night, at Cumberland House, and His Royal Highness returned not thither, from Richmond, till twelve o'clock, it was then too late to think of going to Hayes; but His Royal Highness directed my Lord Albemarle to write immediately to Mr. Pitt, that His Royal Highness would be with him, at Hayes, the next morning, at eleven o'clock; and, to write also to my Lord Temple, that the Duke desired, his Lordship would meet His Royal Highness at Hayes, the next day,[2] at twelve o'clock, His Royal Highness

---

[1] 'Lord Bute's lieutenant.' Cf. *Grenville Correspondence*, iii. 179 *note*. Lord Bute's daughter married the Earl of Northumberland's son, 1764.

[2] May 20. See *Grenville Correspondence*, iii. 39.

being desirous **to see Mr. Pitt alone, for some time, before Lord Temple should come in.**

The Duke as I mentioned, had sent my Lord Albemarle a day or two before to acquaint Mr. Pitt with the situation of things, and what had pass'd with the King, and my Lord Northumberland; and His Royal Highness had seen my Lord Temple twice.

My Lord Albemarle found Mr. Pitt very reasonable, or, at least, much better disposed to take some part, than he ever was afterwards.

Mr. Pitt seem'd highly to approve the method the King had taken, to put this negotiation into His Royal Highness's hands; and said, *It would now do.* He approved also the Duke's having desired the King's leave to consult him (Mr. Pitt), my Lord Temple, the Duke of Newcastle, and the Marquess of Rockingham. He declined indeed being Secretary of State, on account of the uncertainty of his health, and on not knowing what system would be followed in foreign affairs; that, if he was not Secretary of State, but had any other office, which he hinted to my Lord Albemarle he might take, he should not be obliged to insist upon his plan for foreign affairs, (viz. the alliance with the King of Prussia,) being followed.

He commended my Lord Northumberland; but said nothing to what had been mentioned of putting my Lord Northumberland at the head of the Treasury and, I think, mention'd to my Lord Albemarle the three points he should insist upon.

First, restitution to the officers, who had been dismiss'd.[1]

Secondly, that the new Ministers should be allowed, or directed, to propose, in due time, that both Houses should declare the illegality of General Warrants.

Thirdly, that proper measures should be taken for establishing such a connection, or system, upon the Continent, as

---

[1] For their votes in Parliament. Cf. Albemarle's *Rockingham*, i. 193; and for the three points, *Walpole* (Barker), ii. 118.

might oppose the House of Bourbon, in case they should attempt to disturb the publick peace, or should refuse to execute their treaties.

These three points, which were insisted upon to the last, were answer'd in a manner, that, by the account I had of it, I thought, seem'd to be rather satisfactory than otherwise: but, from what I have heard since, I am afraid that was a mistake.

His Royal Highness did not succeed in the two conferences, which he had with my Lord Temple; and both my Lord Temple, and Mr. Pitt agreed, at last, in what was unfortunately the result of the whole.

My Lord Temple would have no dependence at all upon the sincerity of this negotiation; that it was an artful scheme of my Lord Bute's, to get out the present Ministers; that the proposal of putting my Lord Northumberland at the head of the Treasury was a sufficient proof, that my Lord Bute's real design was to be master of the whole, and that he (Ld. Temple) would never have any thing to do, whilst my Lord Bute should remain Minister behind the curtain; and absolutely declined coming in, in any shape whatever.

Mr. Pitt adopted this way of reasoning, afterwards, as will appear by what passed, when His Royal Highness was at Hayes.

I come now to give an account of that conversation.

His Royal Highness was alone with Mr. Pitt, for an hour; afterwards, Lord Temple, and my Lord Albemarle were called in. The substance of what passed, as far as I can recollect the account of it given me both by the Duke of Cumberland, and my Lord Albemarle, was as follows.

His Royal Highness acquainted them, with *all* that had passed with the King, and my Lord Northumberland; with His Majesty's dissatisfaction with his present Ministers, and resolution to part with them; and to form a new administration, (in effect, out of the Opposition,) of which they two were to be the principal parts.

That, as to the three principal points, which had been proposed, viz. the restitution of the officers, the illegality of General Warrants, and a system for foreign affairs, there could be no doubt about them, when once the new administration was settled, and in activity ; and, I think, as I mentioned before, that point went off tolerably well.

But the great affair was, from whence this disposition arose in the King. And both my Lord Temple, and Mr. Pitt, could attribute it to nothing, but my Lord Bute's influence with His Majesty ; and that, while there was any doubt about that, they could have nothing to do ; that the naming my Lord Northumberland was a sufficient proof of it.

His Royal Highness assured them that the thought of my Lord Northumberland was quite over ; and proposed the Treasury to my Lord Temple ; and the Secretary of State, and the conduct of foreign affairs to Mr. Pitt. They both strongly declined coming in ; Mr. Pitt alledging the state of his health ; and both of them, the situation of affairs, which would lay any administration under the greatest difficulty to redress ; and that they did not see clearly enough, into the rise and cause of this disposition in the King, to undertake any thing upon it ; and could not yet form any judgment, what was the cause, or what would be the effect of it.

Great respect, civilities and satisfaction were express'd, in the strongest manner, to His Royal Highness,—for the part he had taken in this affair.

Just at this time, the very extraordinary event of the family reconciliation between Mr. George Grenville and my Lord Temple, in which Mr. Pitt was included, was, unexpectedly to all the world, made, and published ; and Mr. Grenville brag'd of it immediately to the King.

Whether it had any influence, or not, over my Lord Temple, and Mr. Pitt, with regard to their refusal to come in upon what was proposed to them, time must shew. Both parties declared,

I hear, that they were at liberty in regard to their publick behaviour, to act whatever part they should think proper; but, from what was flung out at the same time, it is natural to suppose, that this private, thorough union must, in its consequences, affect their publick behaviour.

Mr. Pitt, I am told, declared to Mr. Grenville, when he first waited upon him, at Hayes, upon the reconciliation, that he (Mr. Pitt) was very glad to see him there; and was rejoiced at the reconciliation of the family: but that 'He beg'd, not one word of publick affairs.'

Upon this answer given by my Ld. Temple and Mr. Pitt to the Duke of Cumberland, His Royal Highness gave over the thoughts of being able to persuade them, to alter their resolution; and was obliged to acquaint the King with it.

His Majesty desired His Royal Highness to see whether some system of administration could not be formed without them. My Lord Egmont would be Secretary of State; Lord Lyttelton might be at the head of the Treasury,[1] with Charles Townshend, Chancellor of the Exchequer; Dowdeswell, Lord John Cavendish and Lord Villiers, or Tom Pelham, the other commissioners.

Lord Lyttelton, and Chas Townshend, both refused; and I particularly objected to my Lord Egmont, as what I knew would make every thing desperate with Mr. Pitt.[2]

And if this plan could ever have been proper to undertake, in any way, it should have been so formed, as to appear only as a summer suit, till Mr. Pitt could come with his winter's dress.[3] In short, it should have been, in my opinion, such a one, as should shew Mr. Pitt, that it was meant to subsist only till he should come, and take the administration upon himself.

---

[1] Cf. *Walpole* (Barker), ii. 122.
[2] Because of his hostility to the Prussian alliance (see below, p. 39).
[3] Compare Charles Townshend's saying (August 1765) that the Rockingham Ministry was 'a lutestring Ministry, fit only for summer wear' (*Chatham Correspondence*, ii. 316).

But, upon the most mature consideration amongst ourselves, we were all unanimously of opinion, that, considering we could neither get Treasurer, nor Secretaries of State ; nor, what was more difficult, find out any one man, who could, or would, take upon him the conduct of the House of Commons, it would be deceiving the King and His Royal Highness to pretend to undertake it.

His Royal Highness then thought it his duty, to acquaint His Majesty with it ; and, going to St. James's for that purpose, he there found the Ministers ; but had no discourse with any of them but my Lord Chancellor,[1] and my Lord Egmont, with whom he had a very long conference.

My Lord Egmont profess'd himself ready to undertake any thing, in any office, and with any person, for His Majesty's service. He express'd his great disapprobation of the present Ministers, and wished any could be found out to succeed them.

My Lord Chancellor was very strong in his opinion, that, at present, that was impossible ; that the spirit on the side of the administration was then so strong in the House of Lords, occasion'd by the tumult of the weavers, that he durst not put the question, upon a royal adjournment ; which, he was sure, would not be agreed to by the House.

This confirmed the Duke of Cumberland in his opinion, that all was over. He went in to the King ; and, after having acquainted the King with the impracticability, he found there was, of forming an administration without Mr. Pitt, he must, in duty, advise His Majesty, to recall (I call it, his old Ministers, in the best manner he could.

He desired my Lord Chancellor, and my Lord Egmont, might be called in, in His Royal Highness's presence ; and after they had said the same thing to the King, which they had before said to the Duke of Cumberland. His Royal Highness

---

[1] Lord Northington.

then advised His Majesty, in their presence, to restore, or continue his Ministers. I think this was Tuesday, the 21st of May.

His Majesty, greatly to his own dissatisfaction, then sent for Mr. Grenville ; and afterwards, the Duke of Bedford ; and acquainted them with his intentions to continue them, and hoped, they would behave better for the future.

Mr. Grenville seem'd pleased ; and the Duke of Bedford express'd much concern for his having displeased the King ; and assured His Majesty, that he would endeavour to avoid it for the future.

They were then to lay before the King, the conditions (I may so call them) upon which they would continue in His Majesty's service ; and Mr. Grenville was to bring them.

The conditions indeed were strong, and made in a most peremptory manner.

First.[1]—That the Marquess of Granby should be declared Captain General, or Commander-in-Chief.

Secondly.—That His Majesty should promise that Lord Bute should not meddle at all in the closet, in any publick affairs.

Thirdly.—That his brother, Mr. Mackenzie, should have nothing to do with the administration of affairs in Scotland ; and should be removed from his office of Keeper of the Privy Seal there.

Fourthly.—That my Lord Holland should be removed from being Paymaster General ; and that, given to Mr. Charles Townshend.

His Majesty told Mr. Grenville often, that he was in their power ; and he must do, what they would have him. He asked Mr. Grenville, whether these were *conditions* ? Mr. Grenville

---

[1] Cf. the conditions in *Grenville Correspondence*, iii. 41, 184 *sqq.* ; *Walpole* (Barker), ii. 125.

answer'd, No, Sir, *questions.* The King asked, are they *sine quâ nons?* Yes, Sir.

The King replied, I will not consent to the first ; I have offer'd my uncle to be Captain General ; and he will accept it, if there should be occasion.

I hear, they affect to give out, that the King's answer was, that his uncle had advised him to keep the army to himself ;[1] and that the naming of Lord Granby, would be an affront, or injury to old Ligonier.[2]

Mr. Grenville, I think, replied, that he did not imagine, His Royal Highness the Duke would have thought of it : but, tho' His Majesty might now be engaged, that might not always remain ; and, would His Majesty think of my Lord Granby then ? The King was much displeased at this perseverance.

As to my Lord Holland, the King said, I don't much like turning [him] out : but, with all my heart, Mr. Grenville.

As to my Lord Bute, I don't remember that the King said any thing. But, as to his brother, Mr. Mackenzie, His Majesty said, as to taking from him the direction of the affairs in Scotland, with all my heart, Mr. Grenville : but do you mean to remove him from his office of Privy Seal ? Yes, Sir.

I am in your hands ; *I must do it* ; and *I will do it* : but I will tell you how that stands. Mr. Mackenzie applied to me to give his office for life. (His Majesty insinuated, he had had enough of that.) The King said, he had refused it : but had promised Mr. Mackenzie, *that he would never turn him out.* After this : Mr. Grenville, I am in your power ; I will do it ; but you will make me do, *as King,* [that] which I should *be a scoundrel* to do, *as a private man.*

[1] Cf. *Walpole* (Barker), ii. 69.
[2] When the Duke of Cumberland fell into disgrace after the convention of Closterseven, Ligonier (b. 1680) succeeded him as Commander-in-Chief (without the title of Captain-General held by the Duke) from October 1757. The Marquis of Granby was at this time high in popular favour, owing to his brilliant generalship in Germany.

N.B. This is represented by some, not to have been said in quite so harsh a manner: but that His Majesty should say: Mr. Grenville, *you make me break my word*.[1] But Mr. Grenville insisted upon it; and my Lord Halifax wrote to my Lord Holland; and my Lord Sandwich to Mr. Mackenzie, to dismiss them from their employments.

It is said, (perhaps in a joke,) that Lord Sandwich asked the King, who should acquaint my Lord Holland? and that His Majesty should answer, *You, my Lord, who turned him out.*

Thus this affair ended, with regard to the continuance of the present Ministers; whose situation I believe, nobody, that knows what business is, and what Ministers should be, can envy; and every true friend to his country must lament the situation, in which the King, and the nation are now in [sic]; and it requires the serious consideration of all the true friends to His Majesty, and the publick, what may be proper to do, upon such an unforeseen and, I believe, unheard of exigency.

I am told that the daily interviews between His Majesty and his Ministers are very disagreeable to both.

The Duke of Cumberland having heard, (I think, from my Lord Lyttelton,) that there was some doubt, about the offer of the Treasury to my Lord Temple, whether it came from the King or not, His Royal Highness desired to see my Lord Temple, my Lord Lyttelton, and my Lord Albemarle. This was, I think, Wensday, May 22.

The little difference, if any, about what had passed was clear'd up to mutual satisfaction; and ended with the Duke of Cumberland's asking my Lord Temple whether, if His Royal Highness was to bring to my Lord Temple an offer of the Treasury directly from the King, he (Ld. Temple) could give him a direct answer?

Lord Temple replied, *No*; he could not, till he had seen Mr. Pitt; that tho' the reconciliation with his brother George

[1] Cf. *Grenville Correspondence*, iii. 187; Walpole's *Letters*, iv. 367.

did not lay him under any obligation or restraint, with regard to their publick behaviour, he (Ld. Temple) might have his delicacies ; and Mr. Pitt might have his delicacies also.[1]

His Royal Highness then, with the greatest fairness, said, if you my Lord Temple, and Lord Lyttelton, will go immediately to Mr. Pitt, (as they did,) and I shall find, at night, that it is still open, with regard to the continuance of the present Ministers, I will then send to you to know Mr. Pitt's answer: But, if I should find that it is over, and that His Majesty should have re-instated his present Ministers, I will not trouble you with sending to you.

When His Royal Highness went back to the King, he found that the Ministers (Mr. Grenville, &c.,) had desisted from their recommendations of Lord Granby, to be Captain General ; and that His Majesty had consented to all their points ; and that, in consequence, the old Ministers were re-instated ; and therefore His Royal Highness did not send to my Lord Temple, as he would have done, if it had been open and the Ministers had not been re-instated.

And thus ended, at that time, this whole affair, to the great disappointment and mortification of all true friends of their country who had been informed of it ; and, after having had in the course of it, at times, the most prosperous appearance.

HOLLES NEWCASTLE.

II

Claremont : June 29, 1765.

Having in the former part of this letter, given you as exact an account, as I could, of the rise, progress, and extraordinary miscarriage of a negotiation for fixing an administration, upon the best, and most solid constitutional principles, to be composed

---

[1] This is the earliest mention of Lord Temple's 'delicacies.' Cf. *Grenville Correspondence*, iii. 65 and *note*.

(as was proposed and hoped) of all the most proper persons, (particularly Mr. Pitt,) from their abilities and characters, and the best intentioned to the true interest of their country, I shall now proceed to acquaint you with many very surprizing circumstances, which have passed since; and am sorry to observe, in the beginning, that, notwithstanding all the offers, concessions, and advances, made by the King himself, and acknowledged by them to Mr. Pitt and my Lord Temple, they have hitherto proved ineffectual, by the refusal of my Lord Temple to come in with Mr. Pitt; tho' His Lordship owns everywhere that the King had offer'd him every thing, and more than he could expect; and, tho' Mr. Pitt had, and does declare his entire satisfaction with every thing that had passed with the King, both as to measures and persons, and his own readiness and desire to come into His Majesty's service: but that he could not do it, if my Lord Temple (which is now unfortunately the case,) should refuse to come in with him.

The rise of this negotiation, as I understand it, was as follows:

On Wensday the 12th instant, the week of the Ascot Races, when the Duke of Grafton and the Marquess of Rockingham were attending His Royal Highness,[1] at Windsor Lodge, the Duke of Bedford had a long audience of the King [2] (the purpose, and design of which was publickly talked of, by His Grace's friends).

His Grace complained in the name of *them* all, of the cool reception they met with from the King; and that His Majesty had no confidence in them. He asked the King's leave, to go to Woburn for a month; and it was supposed that at the end of the month his Grace and his friends would resign, if His Majesty did not alter his behaviour towards them.

Upon this, His Majesty sent to the Duke of Cumberland to

---
[1] The Duke of Cumberland.
[2] *Bedford Correspondence*, iii. 287, 288.

attend him, on Sunday evening following ;[1] and wrote, as I have heard, a very moving letter to His Royal Highness upon it.

His Royal Highness found the King much displeased with his present servants. His Majesty complained of the Duke of Bedford's audience, who spoke for the *whole*, and declared, that if His Majesty did not alter his behaviour to them, by smiling upon them and shewing them more confidence, they could not serve him any longer. His Grace went so far, as to insist, that the King should frown upon those who were in opposition to his Ministers.

The King proposed to His Royal Highness, to try Mr. Pitt again. The Duke named the Duke of Grafton as a proper messenger; which His Majesty approved of; His Grace was expected in town, the next day, and was to go to Hayes, to inform Mr. Pitt, from the King, of the Duke of Bedford's last audience, and to desire Mr. Pitt to come to His Majesty to form an administration.

The Duke of Grafton went that day (Monday) to Hayes, and return'd in the evening. He found Mr. Pitt very lame, with the gout in both his feet; but always *ready, proud* and *in duty bound, to fling himself at His Majesty's feet*, begging to have a day's warning, and a night's rest in London.

The Duke of Grafton could only talk upon general things; as he had no other commission than a message from the King desiring to see Mr. Pitt. His Grace was pleased, upon the whole, with Mr. Pitt's language.

Upon the Duke of Grafton's return from Hayes, His Royal Highness wrote to Mr. Pitt, from Richmond, by the King's order, to be at the Queen's House,[2] on Wensday morning. And the Duke was to see the King, himself, in the evening.

His Royal Highness received on Tuesday evening an answer from Hayes: that he (Mr. Pitt) was *penetrated with the King's condescension*, and *ashamed of the trouble*, His Royal

---

[1] June 16.   [2] Buckingham House, in St. James's Park.

Highness had had on *his account*, but without desiring either to see His Royal Highness before or after his audience. I am well enough acquainted with His Royal Highness, to know, that if the great point is carried, of engaging Mr. Pitt, His Royal Highness will think himself very happy.

Mr. Pitt was between three and four hours with the King, on the Wensday.[1] His conversation was entirely upon measures. In regard to home politicks there was no difference; and he was entirely satisfied and pleased with the King's agreeing to his warmest wishes; particularly with His Majesty's promising Lord Chief Justice Pratt every thing he asked for him at present; not a word of removing the present Chancellor.

His foreign politicks were not thought so reasonable; nor did the King come in to them, viz. a Triple Alliance with Russia and Prussia, which he insisted upon was absolutely necessary, before he could take any part in government.

His Majesty express'd the impropriety of the immediate entering into such measures; that they would be alarming to all Europe and required some consideration; that he could not propose them to his present Ministers; and that, unless Mr. Pitt engaged himself in his service, he could not come into his proposal. His Majesty desired him to consider of it in its full extent, and would see him again.

His Royal Highness was desired to order him (Mr. Pitt) to attend the King again on Saturday. Mr. Pitt was then very shy of naming anybody for employments; talked a little, but not strongly, of Lord Temple for the Treasury; wished Lord Egmont might remain at the head of the Admiralty; mentioned Sir Charles Saunders and Admiral Keppel to be of that Board; proposed Sir George Savile for Secretary at War; wished the Duke of Newcastle President; and that the Duke of Marlborough might be kept in, at any rate.

The Duke of Grafton was sent for, and desired to see Mr.

[1] June 19.

Pitt again before Saturday; and His Royal Highness believed that he would be more explicit; and that it would do on Saturday.

In the audience of Saturday, Mr. Pitt *accepted*,[1] satisfied with the King's telling him, that he was not *averse* to the treaty he proposed with Russia and Prussia, if found practicable upon further consideration of it. No arrangement was settled, or even talked of: but His Majesty was to see Lord Temple, on Tuesday; and immediately after that every thing was to be settled.

My Lord Temple, in his audience of the King, absolutely declined coming into His Majesty's service, for private reasons, which he could not disclose to anybody: but the publick one he gave was, that, in the bad state of Mr. Pitt's health, as he (Ld. Temple) was not in the House of Commons himself, it might frequently happen that Mr. Pitt could not be there; that he could not be sure of Mr. Pitt's assistance in the House of Commons, when perhaps he should be most in need of it; and that he had no other person in the House of Commons upon whom he could entirely depend.[2]

Mr. Pitt has been with the King since, and, as I hear, extremely laments and blames my Lord Temple's refusal; declares his own readiness to come in, and his entire satisfaction: but, as he has had so long a friendship with my Lord Temple; and as they have never once differ'd, in either publick or private affairs; as his ill state of health would frequently prevent him from attending His Majesty, he should, if my Lord Temple was not in His Majesty's service, not have one person, whom he could trust to convey to His Majesty his thoughts upon any occasion wherein he might think His Majesty's service is concern'd.

Thus this great affair stands at present, as far as I have been informed of it.

[1] But compare Pitt's letter, *Grenville Correspondence*, iii. 60.
[2] Cf. *Grenville Correspondence*, iii. 201.

Some time passed after this[1]; and the Duke heard nothing from the King; and it was imagined the reason of that silence was, that His Majesty had still some hopes that Mr. Pitt would change his mind. But in a day or two His Majesty sent for the Duke of Cumberland; and directed him to form a plan of administration, out of such as would serve him.

The Duke of Cumberland immediately sent for us;[2] and the outlines of the plan were consider'd, viz. the Duke of Grafton, and Mr. Charles Townshend, or General Conway, Secretaries of State, the Marquess of Rockingham, at the head of the Treasury, with Mr. Townshend, or Genl Conway, Chancellor of the Exchequer.

Much negotiation and altercation there was, in fixing the Secretary of State and Chancellor of the Exchequer; at last Mr. Townshend peremptorily refused to accept either, declaring his own inclination to accept, but that his brother, my Lord Townshend, would not permit him to do it.[3]

Mr. Conway would by no means be Chancellor of the Exchequer: but, upon Mr. Townshend's refusal, did agree to be Secretary of State; and a very good one he will be.

The other employments were thrown out but nothing absolutely settled, except (I think) my Lord Winchelsea for President of the Council; as I had in the beginning of this negotiation absolutely refused to be President of the Council, when it was offer'd to me.

After His Royal Highness had talked very fully to the

---

[1] On the two negotiations ending the one May 20 and the other June 23, see *Walpole* (Barker), ii. 115-124, 131-3. In the published correspondence of Chatham the two negotiations are scarcely mentioned. Writing July 1 (ii. 316), Pitt alludes to 'this crisis of my life, the most difficult and painful on all accounts which I have ever experienced.' Also (ii. 378) it is stated that Pitt, in the June conference, had refused to acquiesce in Mackenzie's restoration to an office of influence, but consented to his having a sinecure employment.

[2] Grenville did not know of this till July 2 (*Correspondence*, iii. 205).

[3] Cf. *Grenville Correspondence*, iii. 65 *sqq*. Also subsequently, iii. 210. Cf. Walpole (*Letters*, iv. 381, 382), on his vacillations.

Marquess of Rockingham, the Duke of Grafton, (I think,) and myself, I had our principal friends here with me, on the 30th, named in the enclosed list;[1] and you will see by it what passed. There were twelve for forming a new administration, upon consideration of all the circumstances, and six against it,[2] except Mr. Pitt could be prevailed upon to be a part of it.

I went the next day to Windsor Lodge; and found, that the report of what had passed here, the day before, and the opinion given by six of my best friends, that no administration should be formed, except Mr. Pitt was a part of it, had made such an impression upon the Duke, that His Royal Highness had absolutely determined to go, the next day, to the King, and give up the whole, finding, that it was not in his power, to serve His Majesty in this great point, or to form any plan of administration.

I told His Royal Highness, that I hoped he would alter his resolution; that I came on purpose, to persuade him to go on, and form an administration; that I was surprized to see His Royal Highness of that opinion, at a time, when, I thought, we stood upon better ground, than we had ever yet done.

That when the negotiation was on foot, some weeks ago, and Mr. Pitt had then refused, I myself was doubtful, whether it was then advisable or practicable to form an administration with any prospect of success; that the case was very different at present.

That then, tho' very unjustly, it was reported and believed, that there was no real design to have Mr. Pitt in such a situation and with those persons without which he would not or

---

[1] The list is appended to this letter. Cf. *Walpole* (Barker), ii. 134.
[2] The names have been printed in Albemarle's *Rockingham*, i. 218. On this meeting see Charles Yorke's Journal, quoted in Harris's *Hardwicke*, iii. 448: 'All but three or four were for accepting.' His Majesty expressed his wonder at the Duke of Newcastle's asking opinions, and thought that 'he ought to have led their opinions.' 'The Duke of Newcastle listens too much to the younger people, their passions and disgusts.'

could not come; that the negotiation with Mr. Pitt was pure amusement; that Mr. Pitt had then never seen the King; or had had any direct offer from the King to my Lord Temple, or sufficient satisfaction upon measures, either at home or abroad; that, tho' I knew this (as I did) to be false, yet as long as that opinion prevailed, it equally did mischief, and would and did prevent many of our best friends from taking any share in any new administration to be made.

But all that I said was upon a presumption or previous declaration or supposition that some of my Lord Bute's principal friends should be permitted to have any influence or interposition in the management of publick affairs, either at home or abroad, in England or Scotland.

His Royal Highness reflected upon what I had said; and himself was pleased to add, that he saw so much confusion if *we* did not form a new administration, that, as the King would on no account resume again the last administration, viz. the Duke of Bedford, Mr. Grenville, &c., he was assured the King would then think he had no choice but to fling himself absolutely into the hands of my Lord Bute and the Tories.

I also observed, that, at present, [all was] far different from what it was, when His Royal Highness advised the King to resume his old Ministers; Mr. Pitt had in the most generous manner declared his entire satisfaction with what had passed with the King; and that the only reason he did not come into the King's service was that my Lord Temple would not come with him; for which he blamed my Lord Temple extremely. I said, that being the case, if those measures were followed at home and abroad which Mr. Pitt had recommended to the King, and His Majesty had consented to, I was persuaded, so far from giving any opposition, that Mr. Pitt would support them; and I am still of that opinion.

General Conway was present the whole time; and the Marquess of Rockingham came in at last; and I must do them both the justice, that they supported my opinion as strongly as possible.

We then went to the point; and we three entirely agreed in every thing we proposed to His Royal Highness.

The first point was, the removing some of my Lord Bute's friends, and particularly my Lord Despenser, Master of the Great Wardrobe, Lord Bute's most intimate friend. And we pressed extremely the removal of my Lord Litchfield, (Gen[l] Conway and I,) both as a Tory and principal friend of my Lord Bute.[1]

Lord Rockingham had some doubt as to the removal of my Lord Litchfield; as it might make the Tories unanimously take part against us, at the first setting out. But we all agreed that Mr. Mackenzie should not be restored to his office in Scotland; or have any employment whatever, either in England or Scotland, in lieu of it.

It was said, (with what truth I know not,) that Mr. Pitt had consented to the restitution of Mr. Mackenzie as necessary for the King's honor.[2]

It was also agreed to make my Lord Chief Justice Pratt a Peer. There was some difference of opinion whether that should be done immediately or not: but it was agreed afterwards to do it immediately; of which opinion I was most strongly.

His Royal Highness then determined to see Mr. Charles Yorke himself, and to offer him to be Attorney General; and desired my Ld. Rockingham to see Charles Townshend. Mr. Yorke made difficulties, (which, I hope, tho' I don't know it, are by this time removed;) apprehending that it would appear, that Sir Fletcher Norton[3] was removed for the part he took in the prosecution of

---

[1] Cf. Albemarle's *Rockingham*, i. 214 *notes*.

[2] Ultimately Pitt agreed to his restoration (see below, p. 84).

[3] The Attorney-General. In the debate on the resolution declaring the illegality of General Warrants, February 1764, he is reported to have said that 'if I was a

Wilkes ; which might carry with it an imputation upon him for the part which he had had in that transaction.

Lord Hardwicke was offer'd First Lord Commissioner of Trade, which he very civilly declined. Charles Townshend's answer you will have seen in this letter.

To all these points His Royal Highness most readily, and warmly assented ; except to the removal of my Lord Litchfield ; which, however, His Royal Highness promised us to attempt, tho' he fear'd he should meet with difficulties : and all of them are done, except that.

The next point met also with difficulty ; and that was, the making the Duke of Portland Lord Chamberlain, and not the Earl of Northumberland. It was apprehended that also would be attended with difficulty. But we so strongly represented the ill consequence of giving an employment of that dignity, and so near His Majesty's person, to my Lord Northumberland at this time ;[1] and the great satisfaction it would be to us all, and to all the honest men of the Kingdom, to see a man of the Duke of Portland's great consequence, family, fortune, character, and steddiness to the true friends of his country, placed there ; that the Duke, who has the highest opinion of His Grace's distinguished merit, and character, determined to press it to the King, as absolutely necessary for His Majesty's service ; and the King was pleased to consent to it, in the most gracious manner imaginable, with regard to the Duke of Portland.

When the Duke had proposed all these things to the King, His Royal Highness commanded the Duke of Grafton, the Duke of Portland, the Marquess of Rockingham, the Earl of Bessborough, the three Lords Cavendishes,[2] Gen[l] Conway, and

judge I should pay no more regard to this resolution than to that of a drunken porter.' On his removal see *Grenville Correspondence*, iii. 75. Charles Yorke, while condemning the principle of General Warrants, contended that they had been frequently employed (*Lecky*, iii. 161).

[1] He again failed to get the appointment under Grafton's Ministry, July 1766, and was compensated with the dukedom instead.   [2] George, Frederick, and John.

myself, (I think there was nobody else,) to attend him at dinner, at Cumberland House, on Friday, July the 5th.

We there talked over all the several material points, relating to the forming the new administration, the principal Ministers, viz. the Secretaries of State, the Duke of Grafton, and General Conway; the Treasury, that is the Marquess of Rockingham at the head of it; Mr. Dowdeswell to be Chancellor of the Exchequer; the Chancellor to remain; Lord Winchelsea, Lord President; Duke of Newcastle, to be Privy Seal, if the Duke of Marlborough resigned; Lord Talbot to remain Steward; the Duke of Portland, Chamberlain; Lord Egmont at the Head of the Admiralty; Lord Huntingdon, Groom of the Stole; Lord Dartmouth at the Head of the Board of Trade, upon Lord Hardwicke's refusal; and Mr. Charles Yorke, Attorney General in the room of Sir Fletcher Norton.

The other parts of the plan of administration were left to be further consider'd; many have been since filled up and some few are still left undecided.

I then mentioned, at that time, what had been proposed with regard to removing my Lord Litchfield and my Lord Despenser; the latter was immediately agreed to: but some of the Lords doubted whether it would be expedient to attempt to remove my Lord Litchfield just at this time.

I introduced this and the security or assurance to be given us, that my Lord Bute should not be suffer'd to interfere in any part of publick business, or in the disposition of any employments either in England or in Scotland, and particularly that Mr. Mackenzie should not be restored nor any employment be given him in satisfaction for that taken from him; I say I mention'd these points as *sine quâ nons* with us, who declared our opinion at Claremont for forming a new administration.

His Royal Highness declared (I think at that meeting, or I am sure very soon after) that His Majesty had given him the strongest assurances that my Lord Bute should not be suffer'd to interfere in the least degree in any publick business whatever; and that, if those of his friends who might remain in office did not vote with, and, by speaking, support the present administration, His Majesty promised to remove them the next day.

His Royal Highness also added for himself, that he had ventured to tell the King, that, as His Royal Highness had persuaded those who were to come into His Majesty's service, to do so upon the express condition that my Lord Bute should have nothing to do directly or indirectly in publick affairs, if that should appear otherwise, His Royal Highness must himself retire from having any share in His Majesty's affairs, and would not pretend to persuade any one of the King's servants from doing the same and quitting His Majesty's service.

Upon these strong assurances, the present Ministers have accepted their offices; all of us declaring that, whenever there should be the least appearance of my Lord Bute's intermeddling, that we would all then desire His Majesty's leave to resign our employments; and, by the behaviour of all the Ministers and from their declarations and known principles, there is not the least doubt but we shall do so.

Having now introduced the new Ministers into their offices, and having acquainted you with all the previous steps attending it I must conclude this long letter, narrative or journal, with most heartily wishing success to this new, honest, Whig administration, and with assuring you that, upon the principles upon which I have always invariably acted ever since I came into the world, I shall give them all the assistance which either my situation or long, very long experience, (having been thirty years Secretary of State, after an apprenticeship at Court of seven years Lord Chamberlain and eight years at the head of the Treasury,) may have furnished me with.

As I know your long friendship and partiality to me, almost for as many years as I was in publick business, you may be desirous to know some particulars relating to myself which I shall with pleasure give you, as I flatter myself they will meet with your entire approbation, being perfectly conformable to what I have always declared and what you seem'd to wish and desire my conduct should be.

As to myself, His Majesty was pleased early to offer me to be President of the Council; I then desired to be excused, as it was an employment of business, and even a business which was entirely new to me.

When His Majesty commanded me to attend him the day the Ministers were appointed, the King very graciously told me he was glad to see me again in the closet; made me compliments of my zeal &c. for his family. I told him I came to thank him for his gracious offer of the President's place, and gave him my reasons, why I should not accept it.

His Majesty then said, he should have been glad to have had me in a much more considerable office, (meaning, I suppose, at the head of the Treasury,) if he had not known I would not take it.

I told His Majesty I was glad to see those admitted into the first employments in his service who, themselves and their families, had always been sincerely attach'd to His Majesty's Royal Family, and I was persuaded he would see how easy the employing such persons would make his affairs; that I wished His Majesty had had the assistance of Mr. Pitt, but was glad to find that His Majesty had condescended to satisfy Mr. Pitt in every thing, and that Mr. Pitt had been so generous as to declare his satisfaction, and that nothing but my Lord Temple's refusal had prevented him from coming in. And that I was also firmly persuaded that if those measures were pursued which Mr. Pitt had been pleased to recommend to His Majesty, and he had been pleased to approve, ...[1] an . . . . . .[1] Mr. Pitt would support them.

Upon the mention of the Privy Seal, I told His Majesty

[1] The copyist seems to have found this passage illegible.

I should be very ready and thankful to take it, if the Duke of Marlborough quitted it, but that I should be very sorry to deprive His Majesty of the service of one of the most considerable subjects he has, and who was of the family and bore the name of Marlborough, to which I had been attach'd ever since I was born.

His Majesty was graciously pleased to say, that he desired I would undertake the Church affairs,[1] that is, the recommending to all Church preferments. I told His Majesty, with the assistance of the Archbishop of Canterbury I should obey His Majesty's commands; that my part had always been to recommend no one who had not these two qualifications:—

First, that he should always be one of a good, unblemish'd life and character, and such as one of his profession ought to be.

Second, that he should be, and should have always been, most zealously attach'd to the protestant succession in his Royal Family.

His Majesty seem'd to approve what I said, and was very gracious during the whole audience. I have had one audience of the King since, in which every thing passed very well.

The King sent for the Archbishop of Canterbury and acquainted His Grace with what his intention was, with regard to the disposition of all ecclesiastical preferments.

It is now time to put an end to this long journal, and indeed I have nothing more to add than that I am, what I have been for forty years, dear Sir, your most affect^e friend, and most obliged and obedient humble servant,

HOLLES NEWCASTLE.

---

[1] Mr. Lecky (iii. 94) says that the Duke obtained the Church patronage at his own desire.

Fo. 30.

III

[Here follows a note of the meeting at Claremont, June 30, 1765, which has been published in Albemarle's 'Life of Rockingham,' i. 218-220, and is therefore here omitted. It is transcribed for Mr. White at Newcastle House, July 31, 1765. It contains a list of eighteen persons who protested against the restoration of Mr. Mackenzie. The twelve in favour of joining a new administration are named, and the six against.]

IV

Fo. 32.   Claremont : December 3, 1765.

MY DEAR OLD FRIEND,—Your letter of the 25th of last month gave me the greatest pleasure, as you say in it, what I know without your saying it, that it was rather too late (for you) to go out of the *old track*. The knowledge of that and the many proofs I have had of your most valuable friendship, the great want I have of the advice of a true, intelligent friend, at a time when Providence has deprived me of the most able and valuable one that ever man had (I mean my Lord Hardwicke,[1]) and the behaviour of others has put them out of the capacity of being of that use to me which I had reason formerly to expect from them—I say, lay me under the greater necessity of troubling those few that are left, who are willing and able to advise me, and, who will believe the facts as I state them, as far as they regard myself.

Yourself and my good friend my Lord Grantham are the chief friends on whom I can now depend. I have had great friendly assistance from that worthy man my Lord Bessborough, but, without troubling you with a list of ungrateful men of which I am sorry to say I find more *now*, since the establishment of *an administration of friends*, than ever I did before, during the

[1] Died March 6, 1764.

Opposition, when it might have been thought by lookers-out that I should have more weight with the next administration than appears now to be the case.

Without troubling you, I say, with a long list, I shall only acquaint you with what I conclude you must know, that my Lord Lincoln, the son of my favourite sister, my nephew and heir, never comes near me and has broke off all correspondence with me. The two causes alledged are, that I did not oblige old Mr. Wilkinson, and force his son, (which he could not do,) to sell his burgage houses in Boroughbridge to my Lord Lincoln; and, if he would not do it, that I should not have done him justice, in restoring him to his place in the Ordnance, from which he was removed singly for adhering to me.

The next cause assigned is, that I did not make him Lord Lieutenant of Nottinghamshire. I sent to offer him Sherwood Forest, as it was contiguous to Clumber where he was laying out so much money; *that* he refused, except he could have the Lieutenancy also. I talked it, as I thought, friendlily over with him. He said I had yielded Sussex to the Duke of Richmond, had not accepted Middlesex,[1] and why would I insist upon Nottingham?[2] I gave my reasons for the other two, and said, But why will you leave me nothing? If I take it myself, nobody can be angry with me, but why will you force *me* to disoblige either the Duke of Kingston or the Duke of Portland? Upon which he fell into a fury and said, the Duke of Kingston would wish that he, Lord Lincoln, might have it, but that this was preferring the Duke of Portland to him. That was so unreasonable that there I left it, and I have not seen His Lordship since.

Having premised thus much with regard to myself, I shall, in the same confidence with which I communicated to you all the previous steps, which I could recollect, to the forming the

---
[1] It went to the Earl of Northumberland
[2] The Duke of Newcastle became Lord Lieutenant, September 7, 1765

present administration, in my letter to you of July 31st,[1] now acquaint you with the present state of the administration, and the most material things which have passed since they came in ; and particularly (which I hope you will seriously consider) the part that I have and am to act in it.

The putting my Lord Rockingham at the head of the Treasury, and thereby the making him first Minister, was done without my immediate knowledge, but very much with my approbation, for I profess to you, now, he is the person in all England I wish there.

The office of Privy Seal is the only one I would take, as I thought it answer'd all my purposes and those of my friends ; I thought it gave me an opportunity of serving in some measure that cause which I ever had and ever will support, without subjecting me either to the trouble, fatigue or responsibility of a Minister: but little did I think that these young men, and particularly my Lord Rockingham would take any one material step in government either with regard to measures or men, without previously consulting me or knowing my thoughts, and *that* they would not do, if they either had that regard for my opinion, which, from vanity, I may think they should have, or in their situation thought they wanted my assistance.

When this Ministry was first establish'd, my Lord Rockingham and the Duke of Grafton both came to me and told me they should want my advice in every thing ; that they were quite strangers ; that every thing was new to them, &c. I told them very truly, whenever they wanted it and desired it, I was always at their service. The King (don't think I depend upon Kings entirely,) talked always the same language and does so still. When I commend these new Ministers, His Majesty always shows great approbation of them, but he said to me,

---

[1] No. III is so dated, but it would seem that a letter accompanied it which is now missing.

they are young, they must have your advice, &c. To which I said once for all, whenever your Majesty or your Ministers wish to have my opinion, you shall have it to the best of my understanding. But I shall not think that I have any pretension to insist upon its being followed if it differs from the opinion of those Ministers who are to have the execution, and are to be responsible for the measure.

Would you imagine that after this my Lord Rockingham has scarce once spoken to me, or not above once, about any measure to be taken by the Treasury? But, on the contrary, by a total and cruel exclusion of poor West,[1] after he himself had proposed to bring him into the Treasury, by restoring him to his old place, and afterwards making him a Lord of the Treasury, has left him, mark'd out as an unfit object: which is no great credit to those who have employed him for so many years; and by every act of the Treasury it appears that those gentlemen are setting out upon a new plan, and are afraid of being thought to be influenced or advised by *any of their predecessors*. This I attributed at first to your friend Mr. Mellish,[2] who has now prefer'd a very beneficial office which I gave him, unask'd, to all the emoluments he could propose from Treasury favour.

I also attribute a great deal of the behaviour of the Treasury towards me to my old, ungrateful, *conceited* friend Sir William Baker,[3] who thinks he can entirely govern these young men, and to some *fashionable young lords* and gentlemen who are shewing every day that they prefer the favor of a young man who may serve them to that of an old man who has always served them and their cause.

The truth is my Lord Rockingham and the Duke of Grafton think themselves so sure of the closet, that they neglect every other consideration; they make up their majorities in both

---

[1] James West, who had been in the Treasury, 1760-1.

[2] William Mellish, Secretary to the Treasury.

[3] M.P. See *Grenville Correspondence*, ii. 457; Walpole's *Letters*, iv. 179.

Houses, and are more solicitous to gain new friends than oblige and retain their old ones.

As to their intentions for the good of the publick and the constitution, I am clear they are as good as possible; that they will act extremely well in their respective offices and make themselves masters of it; but, that is not *sufficient alone* to constitute a Minister, who shall have the care and conduct of the affairs of this vast kingdom at home and abroad, in Scotland, Ireland, Africa and America; that can be got by nothing but time and experience.

They will feel and perhaps soon, tho' they don't seem to be the least apprehensive of it, the loss of that great and meritorious Prince the Duke of Cumberland.[1] You see the universal sense of the nation upon this melancholy event. Everybody, that wished well, looked up to him; they knew that to him singly we owed the happy turn taken, the removal of the late Ministers and the establishment of the present; and the generality of men not depending so much upon the stability of court favour, as these young Ministers do, looked up to the Duke as the only person who would, who could interpose, to keep the court steddy to these men and those measures which he had brought them to, upon any appearance of a disposition to change.

As soon as His Royal Highness died, I went immediately to the King, without the knowledge and concert of any of the Ministers, and told His Majesty that as an old servant of his family, I should take the liberty to tell him freely my opinion upon that great and melancholy event; that His Majesty had lost a most affectionate friend and most able and faithful subject; that everybody did look up to him. His Majesty seem'd entirely to approve what I said. I added that it would be to His Majesty's honor to shew the utmost regard to his

---

[1] He died October 31, 1765.

memory, which he very readily came into. I then told him that there was a *charm* which must be supplied, to which the King most readily agreed. The particulars of that whole transaction you will find in the enclosed letters to which therefore I refer you.[1]

The publick measures and private ones which seem'd to be agreed to so unanimously amongst us all are either suspended or totally laid aside, without any previous concert amongst us. The alliance with Prussia, so much, in appearance, desired by everybody but my Lord Egmont, totally dropt; improper and, in my opinion, humiliating excuses made to the court of Vienna; indications of a desire to adopt a different foreign system; and, above all, no farther thought of an application to Mr. Pitt, when it appears to me more wanted than ever: however, you will see my thoughts at large upon these subjects, as well as my doubts and apprehensions about my Lord George Sackville.[2]

I have thus flung out my thoughts to you in the utmost confidence and secrecy. I must beg when you come to town, that you will open yourself fully and unreservedly upon every article of this letter; and, to encourage you to do it with greater freedom, I do most solemnly declare to you, that I shall be rejoiced to find that you differ with me, (if that should be the case,) in every material part of this letter, and particularly in those parts which relate singly to myself.

I desire nothing but thorough friendship, confidence and previous concert from my Lord Rockingham; it is him I mean principally. I love him; and if he shews that opinion of me he ought to have, and shews it essentially, as I have said in my letter, I will be a faithful and an useful friend to him. I have not yet lost all my credit in this country, and particularly with the Whigs.

---

[1] Not found.
[2] Disgraced by court martial 1760, and restored 1764. The Vice-Treasurership of Ireland was offered to him. See below, p. 41.

You are the only man that I think can do this. I give you *full powers*; you shall settle the terms, and you shall be the judge of the execution on each side. Believe me, I am in earnest in every part of this letter; but I will add one word more; if I find all my sincere declarations and the endeavours and representations of my best friends shall not be able to set matters right, I shall not long consent to be called to formal meetings, and consulted with my Lord Chancellor, and my Lord Egmont, upon things perhaps settled in some measure before, without being in the full and previous confidence of my Lord Rockingham; for, as to the other two, I honor, respect and love them; but my acquaintance with them is very late in comparison with that of my Lord Rockingham.

It hurts me to be put by this administration in point of confidence and communication upon a foot with my Lord Chancellor and my Lord Egmont, and perhaps *after them*. And so you may tell my Lord Rockingham. Pray weigh this letter; you have time to do it, for I don't expect any answer till I see you.

I beg you would make my kindest compliments to our good friend Mr. Hewett;[1] I hope, and don't doubt, but he will be at the House, on the 17th. I own I have a more than ordinary desire that those friends of mine who do honor to our cause, should appear the first day of the session. I hear the Duke of Bedford has summoned all his friends; so I suppose we shall have some opposition, as I always imagined, to the Address; tho' both the Speech and Address, I hear, are to be very innocent.

I have reserved for the last, to tell you the good news that the Dutchess of Newcastle is returned from Bath, I thank God purely well; she sends her best compliments to you.

I am, my dear friend, &c.,

HOLLES NEWCASTLE.

[1] John Hewett, M.P. for Nottinghamshire.

P.S.— There is one ill consequence I apprehend from the numbers, we are endeavouring to get, of those who composed the two last administrations, that it may make *us* less zealous in pushing some national points on which we insisted so much in the Opposition, lest we should not have the concurrence of some of those gentlemen, and thereby our majority be lessen'd. My view, and I hope that will be the case, is, that this administration should not only be supported by *court favor*, (precarious in all times,) but by their credit and weight in the kingdom, and by shewing the uprightness and steddiness of their conduct, of which as far as relates to themselves, I have no doubt.

If you see Sir George Savile,[1] I beg you would assure him of my most sincere respects, and that I hope to see him perfectly well and in spirits, at the opening of the session.

I have already taken the necessary steps to obey your commands about your nephew Sir Griffith Baynton.

HOLLES NEWCASTLE.

Newcastle House : December 5, 1765.

P.S.—Since writing my letter I have had two conversations with my Lord Rockingham ; they were both very friendly, especially the last : but I can't say that I found any very material alteration with regard to his behaviour towards me in business. I saw but too plainly that they think no other opinion necessary, but that of themselves, viz. Lord Rockingham, the Duke of Grafton, and Gen¹ Conway ; that was the case of the final resolution taken, to offer the Vice Treasurer of Ireland to Lord George Sackville ; which was agreed, without my knowing that it was determined, tho' I had often . . . . been mention'd amongst us, when neither my Lord Rockingham nor myself had declared our consent to it. Some, and those very unlucky, things relating to our foreign affairs have been done, contrary I think to our plan of foreign affairs.

[1] M.P. for Yorkshire.

However, all this may be set right, I hope, by you. I am sincere in all I have said to you.

I don't doubt but these Ministers will have, (as I am sorry to say now, all Ministers will have,) majorities in both Houses of Parliament, and on that our young friends do found their hopes and their security: but that in my opinion proceeds from the worst of causes, the certainty of *any court* carrying any points.[1] Numbers we are sure of; but weight, credit, and real reputation in the kingdom must arise from *conduct*, and from due regard shew'd to persons of weight and experience. However I have troubled you too much, and shall only add the assurance of being ever,

My dear old friend, &c.,
HOLLES NEWCASTLE.

V

Fo. 39 b.   Claremont: December 15, 1765.

DEAR SIR,—I have just now read over my long letter to you of the 3rd, to see whether there was any the least alteration in our circumstances or in my own situation; I am sorry to tell you there is none.

The publick events are of such consequence, that for the present I shall not think of myself, but give the best advice when called upon; and the warmest support in my power to the present Ministers. My Lord Rockingham has not so much as desired my assistance in the House of Lords; he depends upon my Ld. Chancellor[2] and my Lord Egmont for his supports. A strange phænomenon! I hear the Duke of Bedford, George Grenville, Lord Temple, with some stragglers of my Lord Bute's and my Lord Holland's are to make the Opposition.

[1] Walpole traced the increase of court power to the collapse of parties (Barker), ii. 270).
[2] Lord Northington.

I don't withdraw the full power I have given you; and hope to see you early on Tuesday morning.

Ever yours,
HOLLES NEWCASTLE.

VI

Fo. 40. Claremont: January 9, 1766.[1]

MY DEAR FRIEND,— I must trouble you upon all occasions till something is determined upon the present most embarrassing situation of things, and I beg you would communicate this letter to the Duke of Portland.

I went yesterday to court and executed my plan. I found that my Lord John[2] had either not seen or not given my Lord Albemarle's letter to my Lord Rockingham; or that His Lordship had suppressed it, which I rather believe.

I found at St. James's, my Lord Chancellor and my Lord Rockingham together; the two Secretaries were then in with the King; my Lord Chancellor had been in with His Majesty and had, by his own relation, talked very properly to His Majesty, and with great goodness and respect to me; and had particularly said to the King, how cruel this exclusion was upon me, who had accepted this office *only* by His Majesty's command, and not from any inclination of my own.

My Lord Rockingham said little then; seem'd grave; had received my letter, said nothing upon it, but appear'd to be in the same sentiments and disposition that he was in the night before.

The Duke of Grafton gave me a full account of all that had passed with the King, the purport of which was that the day before he had accepted the office of Secretary of State, he had promised Mr. Pitt whenever he (Mr. Pitt) was disposed to come

---

[1] Cf. a letter from Newcastle of the same date to Lord Rockingham, Albemarle's *Rockingham*, i. 264.
[2] Lord John Cavendish.

into the King's service, he (the Duke of Grafton) would resign his employment to him; that he, having made no condition or exception to Mr. Pitt, thought himself obliged in honor and conscience to leave his employment whenever Mr. Pitt was disposed to come into the King's service, that that being now the case, tho' he much disapproved the *two conditions* relating to my Ld. Rockingham and myself,[1] he thought himself not at liberty to remain Secretary of State, if Mr. Pitt was not in the King's service when he was ready to come in. You may imagine I said nothing either to confirm or dissuade His Grace from acting according to his own opinion.

My Lord Rockingham then went in to the King. I don't know so correctly what passed with my Lord Rockingham as what had passed with the Duke of Grafton and Mr. Conway, of which His Majesty was pleased to give me a most minute account, and was in a hurry to do it before I could even execute my intention. His Majesty seem'd much to lament the Duke of Grafton's resolution, and enter'd very minutely into His Grace's reasons, and strongly combatted every one of them. The King seem'd not to think Mr. Conway was in the same disposition.

His Majesty was most gracious to me, and particularly upon the part I was then taking. He read my Paper[2] *to himself* and wanted to keep it, as he was pleased to say, as a proof of the very generous part that I was taking out of regard to him and his service: but said, his own honor was concern'd in this point with regard to me and my Lord Rockingham.

Upon talking over the matter fully and upon my acquainting him with my having wrote to my Lord Rockingham that morning,[3] the King said that he would not send for Mr. Pitt to come to him, (for that was the point labour'd by the Duke of Grafton,

---

[1] Cf. *Walpole* (Barker), ii. 183. The two conditions were the exclusion of the Duke of Newcastle and the offer of the Treasury to Lord Temple.

[2] Here in the margin is a reference, 'Vid. Append. Page.' These appendices have not been found.   [3] Albemarle's *Rockingham*, i. 265.

and, upon certain conditions, supported by Mr. Conway). The King said to me, I will not send for Mr. Pitt without telling him *that I will not consent to his two conditions*, for, if I say nothing, Mr. Pitt will think that I consent to *them*.

His Majesty said little of what had passed with my Lord Rockingham : but the King wished, as I think very rightly, to gain time, as the Duke of Grafton seem'd to press that some resolution should be taken this day.

The Duke of Grafton was extremely civil to me, and said he did not intend to quit immediately; he would go thro' the business of his office, but would not appear to intend to continue there or to act as a Minister, but purely to do the duty of his office. The King told my Lord Chancellor that Mr. Pitt, *he knew*, was very ungrateful to me.

When I came out of the closet I told the two Secretaries that I had executed my plan and that His Majesty was very gracious to me. I then, or I think rather, before I went into the closet, shew'd them my paper, which they both approved. My Lord Rockingham made an alteration in my paper, and after the words, to fix or form an administration to your Majesty's satisfaction, I had put it <u>and to that of the Publick</u> : he struck out those words underlined, which, he said, were too great a compliment to Mr. Pitt, and so the words were out.

I had a great deal of discourse afterwards with my Lord Rockingham : Mr. Conway I think was present some little time with my Lord Rockingham, and I find Mr. Conway's plan is that the King should send for Mr. Pitt and then declare to him that he cannot agree to Mr. Pitt's two conditions.

I found my Lord Rockingham under great doubt and uneasiness. His Lordship seem'd mightily to want to know the sentiments of our own friends, whether Mr. Pitt should come in or not upon his own terms. The Duke of Grafton had said that many of those who had taken employments did it, as His Grace had done, that Mr. Pitt should come in whenever he himself should be disposed to do it, (and, I suppose, it is meant upon his own terms,) and that therefore they would all be displeased and disappointed if it was not now done. This makes my Lord Rockingham desirous to know the opinion of our friends.

I have the greatest reason to think that my Lord Rockingham had had a very private conversation with *my friend* Mr. Charles Yorke, yesterday morning, before I saw His Lordship at court, and I think, in my present circumstances *at least*, my Lord Rockingham should not have kept it a secret from me. I have my suspicions; my friend Mr. Yorke (another of my grateful friends,) may have advised my Lord Rockingham to acquiesce and consent to Mr. Pitt's coming in; as Mr. Yorke has never said one word to me upon the subject; and, as I suspect, my Lord Rockingham concealed from me his having seen Mr. Yorke, yesterday morning, and my Lord Rockingham was certainly less determined yesterday when I left him near five o'clock than he was the night before.

If my suspicions about Charles Yorke are true, he must be *ungrateful* indeed, for I am persuaded that at this instant one of Mr. Pitt's great and perhaps the greatest objection against me, is his apprehension of my concurring with the King's known inclination to prefer Mr. Yorke to my Lord Camden, which [1] I suppose is one of Mr. Pitt's first objects and indeed the principal one.

I have desired you to show this letter to the Duke of Portland. If you meet with my Lord Grantham I could wish he may see it. And I have no objection to Lord John's [2] seeing it, who I desire should know and approve every step I take. As my suspicions of Charles Yorke are only conjectures, I could wish my Lord Rockingham may not know that part of my letter.

Pray send me a line, to come by to-morrow's fishman [3] from

---

[1] *I.e.* Lord Camden's appointment to the Chancellorship.
[2] Lord John Cavendish.
[3] Perhaps as being safer than the post.

Newcastle House, what news you can pick up, and what use you have or may intend to make of this letter.

I am, my dearest friend,
Ever most affectionately yours,
HOLLES NEWCASTLE.

VII

Fo. 43 b.   Newcastle House: February 27, 1766.

Some remarkable occurrences which have happen'd of late at court and in Parliament.

On Tuesday the 4th instant, the day on which the resolutions relating to the Stamp Act were under consideration, there was a question whether the Lords should address the King *to recommend* or *require* the Colonies[1] to make satisfaction to the sufferers, &c.

My Lord Le Despenser spoke very strongly for the enforcement of the Stamp Act and for obliging the Colonies to pay the arrears. This was the first appearance in the House of Lord Bute or his friends taking any open part in opposition to the administration. We divided upon the question and lost it by three votes, 60 for the word *recommend*, 63 for *require*.

This and some other incidents of the same kind which happen'd in the House of Commons made the Ministers think it was necessary to consult their friends upon the part they (the Ministers) should take in their present circumstances; and, accordingly, I was desired to be at the Duke of Grafton's the next morning, where, to the best of my remembrance, were the Duke of Grafton, the Duke of Portland, the Marquess of Rockingham, Lord Winchelsea, Lord Albemarle, Lord Dartmouth, Lord Egmont, Lord Bessborough, Gen[l] Conway, (I think Lord John Cavendish, but I am not certain) and myself.

---

[1] Cf. *Walpole* (Barker,, ii. 201.

The consideration before us was, whether the Ministers upon these appearances should then resign their employments or not? The Duke of Grafton was for their resigning immediately. I gave my opinion most strongly against it and gave my reasons, which were, that as the Repeal of the Stamp Act was now actually under consideration, and as that was in my opinion such an essential point to this country, if the Ministers should then quit their employments, and the Bill for the Repeal should, as it probably would in that case, miscarry, the whole blame of the miscarriage would be imputed to them; that therefore the Ministers should go on, not shewing the least appearance of any intention to resign, or suspicion of their not remaining in full power, and credit; that they should have but one view, to do every thing in their power to carry the Bill for the Repeal; that if they succeeded it would be a proof of their strength, if not they had done their part and, in either case, then and not till then, would be the proper time for them to consider what part they should take either for resigning or strengthening their administration. That as to myself, my part was taken, that I had already told the King that my remaining in my employment depended upon my Lord Rockingham's situation; if His Lordship thought he could remain with credit and a proper degree of power at the head of the Treasury, I would remain with him but if His Lordship, with whom I was connected, both acting upon the same principles and with the same views, should think he could no longer be of service to His Majesty, and to the cause in which we were engaged, I should then desire the King's leave to resign my employment.

My opinion against the administration resigning their employments and the reasons I gave for it were universally applauded by all the company but the Duke of Grafton.

I went immediately with the same view to the Queen's House; I found Lord Egmont with the King. Soon after my Lord Chancellor came in, who had been sent for. The Duke of

Grafton had been there but was gone, and my Lord Rockingham came in after the Chancellor.

I saw nothing of my Lord Egmont. My Lord Chancellor said he had been sent for by the King; he talked in a general way, that things were in great confusion, that an administration should be formed out of the best of the parties &c. The King sent for my Lord Chancellor; he was about half an hour with His Majesty. Lord Rockingham and I just saw him; we found he had talked to the King in the same general way which he had done to us.

His Majesty then ordered me to come to him. I began by making an excuse for troubling him, on a day when I found he had order'd his Ministers to attend him: but that after what had passed in parliament, I could not avoid paying my duty to him. The King was pleased to say he was glad to see me, was desirous to know my thoughts &c.—and did intend to send for me. That being over I acquainted His Majesty that I was very ready to give him my opinion; but that previous to that I beg'd leave to ask three questions; to which His Majesty very graciously replied, I will answer them very truly, I assure you.

1st. The first question, Sir, which I should humbly hope to know is whether your Majesty has any plan or any desire or wish or any intention to form a new administration?

No, I have not.

2nd. The second question, Sir, whether your Majesty wishes to continue and support your present Ministers?

Yes, if it can be done.

3rd. The third, whether your Majesty is for the Repeal of the Stamp Act?

Yes, I am now. I was not for it at first, but now I am convinced or think *that* is necessary.

Why then, Sir, I will humbly lay before your Majesty my thoughts upon the present situation.

I am humbly of opinion that all endeavours should be used to carry the Repeal of the Stamp Act; that at present that should be the only point in view; that the carrying the repeal would be very agreable to the nation, and give weight and strength to your Majesty's administration; and that I hoped your Majesty would let your servants know your opinion upon it.

His Majesty was pleased to say, he had done so. 'But what can I say when they tell me they can't in conscience vote for the Repeal?' To which I replied, 'Conscience, Sir, is too often influenced by prejudice in favour of persons and things, and that courts have ways of letting their opinion be known.'

I then took the liberty to show His Majesty the names of the Lords who voted against us, of which there were between thirty and forty that either had actually employments or were under the influence of the court. His Majesty instanced in [*sic*] my Lord Talbot and my Ld. Denbigh to whom he had spoke; and had thought at first that my Lord Talbot would not have been against the Repeal, but that His Lordship told him since that he must in conscience be against the Repeal; that my Lord Denbigh would be against it but he would not speak.

His Majesty, who *seem'd* surprized at some names in the list, said, that he would *speak*, but did not imagine that he should be able to do much. When the fate of the Repeal should be over, I told His Majesty then would be the time for His Majesty to settle his administration, and to consider whether any or what additional strength could or should be got to his administration.

I think it was in that conversation, or, I am sure, in one about that time, I told the King in talking about forming an administration that I had no resentment to the person I was hinting at;[1] but I knew he was honor'd with His Majesty's favor;

---

[1] This may be Pitt, for Newcastle was no longer 'earnest for Pitt' as he had been hitherto, because he now knew of Pitt's bitter personal hostility to himself. See below, p. 54.

that I would presume to say, that if any administration should be composed of his particular friends or in a manner to be influenced by him, he himself would be the first man in the Kingdom *to repent it*. His Majesty seem'd struck with what I said ; but it went off and he was very gracious to me when I left him.

On Thursday the 6th of Feb'y my Lord Bute made that extraordinary speech in support of the Stamp Act ;[1] in which he said he was of that opinion, tho' the King (of whom he spoke with the utmost duty and gratitude) should be of another.

Many differ'd about the interpretation of that speech. Some thought it was a vanity to shew His Lordship would act according to his conscience, tho' it should be against what His Majesty wished. I and many others thought (and, I think, the event proves it,) that it was to shew that he really knew His Majesty's opinion and therefore acted as he did.

The next day, I think, Friday the 7th of Feb'y was that great division in the House of Commons, where we carried it against the Address, proposed by Mr. Grenville, for enforcing the Stamp Act, by a very great majority. The numbers were 274 to 134.

This made my Lord Bute probably consider what was to be done, and some new turn must be taken or something done or they could have no chance to fling out the Repeal. Lord Strange was sent for or went in to know the King's pleasure about the Repeal of the Stamp Act.[2] His Lordship reported that His Majesty told him, he was for *modification* and not *repeal* ; and that he (Ld. Strange) was authorized by the King to say so ; and that His Majesty's inclination *had been misrepresented.*

Lord Rockingham hearing that and having himself had the

---

[1] Cf. *Walpole* (Barker), ii. 200.
[2] See *Rockingham*, i. 300 ; *Walpole* (Barker), ii. 205.

King's leave to declare that His Majesty was *for the Repeal* thought himself concerned to have this matter clear'd up, and procured His Majesty's consent to a paper left with the King,[1] that His Majesty had authorized my Lord Rockingham to say that he was *for the Repeal*, added in the King's own hand— *there having been that day no discourse between them but* REPEAL *or* ENFORCE. So this affair ended with my Lord Rockingham.

As I had reported also, and I thought I had plainly understood the King, that His Majesty was for the repeal, I thought it my duty to acquaint the King that I had done so, as I understood His Majesty to have said so, and that I thought it for His Majesty's service that it should be known.

His Majesty was very gracious, and said he was for *modification* rather than either *repeal* or *enforce*: but that he was incapable of thinking that either my Lord Rockingham or I would misrepresent him. Thus this affair went on. The numbers in all previous questions in the House of Commons were for the Repeal, and at last the Repeal was carried in the House of Commons by a vast majority; 275 for the Repeal, and I think 167 against it.

The Archbishop of Canterbury, upon the uncertain reports relating to His Majesty's declaration, upon this occasion, thought it his duty to go to the King, and after declaring his own opinion for the Repeal received from His Majesty an assurance that His Majesty was for the *Repeal*, of which the Archbishop made very good use with the Bench.

There were many very long and fine debates in the House of Lords upon the question on both sides; and particularly from my Lord Mansfield and my Lord Camden who both spoke most incomparably well. I think the strength of the argument was greatly with my Lord Camden. The House divided

---

[1] See *Rockingham*, i. 300; *Walpole* (Barker), ii. 205.

upon the main question, proxies and all for the Repeal 105, against, 71.

Thus ended this debate. There was another in the House of Lords upon the Repeal of the Cyder Tax, upon which there was no division. My Lord Mansfield and I spoke strongly for the Repeal of the Cyder Act,[1] my Lord Mansfield most incomparably and most judiciously well. I took an occasion to justify the late war, and to do justice to those who had conducted it with so much ability and success; and that all had been obtained by it for the honor and interest of this country *that could be obtained by war*. I mentioned also the justice, propriety and effect of the additional taxes upon malt and beer for the effectual support of that war.

My Lord Lyttelton and my Lord Temple were both for the Repeal of the Cyder Act, my Lord Sandwich against it. The Duke of Grafton spoke strongly for the Repeal and took occasion from an expression of my Lord Sandwich's, to make a long encomium upon Mr. Pitt and to express the wishes and hopes of all companies he went into, and of the whole Nation, that Mr. Pitt should come into the King's service.

My Lord Sandwich denied that it was the wish of all companies or of the majority of the Nation. He asserted the contrary, and that he did not know what company the Duke of Grafton kept: but he believed it was not the wish of above *one* or *perhaps* two of those with whom it was to be supposed that His Grace was the most connected. What Lord Sandwich meant by this extraordinary assertion I am at a loss to know.

Having now mentioned Mr. Pitt, tho' I have in several of my letters to Mr. White given an account of all that has passed with Mr. Pitt, the King, Lord Rockingham and the Duke of Grafton, upon my subject, I join to this Narrative my letter to the Duke of Grafton, of Nov\u1d63 6th last past, and the paper I sent [2]

---

[1] Passed by Lord Bute.
[2] There is a marginal reference to a letter of January 8, 1766, in Appendix (lost).

and left with His Majesty upon the account given me by Mr. Tho⁵ Townshend Jun⁷ of what had passed between Mr. Pitt and him upon my subject.

The several letters and papers will shew beyond any possibility of contradiction, how earnest I had been from the beginning, for bringing Mr. Pitt into the King's service, and particularly how strongly I pressed it, and how far I had succeeded with the King, immediately upon the ever-to-be-lamented death of that great Prince, His Royal Highness, the Duke of Cumberland. How far I had succeeded with the King, how much I concluded the Duke of Grafton had or would write, agreably to what His Grace had proposed himself and promised, and how strongly I pressed His Grace to do it in my letter of Nov⁷ the 6th last past, to which letter I never to this day have had any answer, those letters will also shew.

It was indeed very remarkable that after my Lord Rockingham and the Duke of Grafton knew how earnest I had been about Mr. Pitt's coming in, they should send my own nephew young Mr. Thomas Townshend down to Mr. Pitt, in the name only of my Lord Rockingham, the Duke of Grafton and Mr. Conway, without saying one single word of me.

The total omission of my name upon this occasion, and some circumstances relating to me in some letters which had passed between Mr. Pitt, Mr. Tho⁵ Walpole and Mr. Nuttal, Solicitor to the Treasury, (some of which were of so long a date as the beginning of Nov⁷,[1] of which I had never heard one word, till Sir Geo. Colebrooke was so good as to inform me of it, on Wensday Jan⁷⁵ the 22d,) might give Mr. Pitt some handle : but he should have inquired into the truth of his suspicions, before he made such an unjust condition of his coming into the King's service, *that he could not sit at Council with the Duke of Newcastle.*[2] Such harsh terms can never be justified, and I think

---

[1] Cf. *Chatham Correspondence*, ii. 328-349.
[2] See *Walpole* (Barker), ii. 163.

ought to have been taken up at first with a high hand, or my nephew Mr. Townshend should have excused himself from carrying such a message to the Ministers, so offensive to his own uncle; and I am of opinion that if the Ministers, and in that I think all three should have joined, had taken it up at first as they should have done, Mr. Pitt would not have adhered to it.

My Lord Rockingham, the Duke of Grafton and Mr. Conway have jointly and separately seen Mr. Pitt, the two last and especially the Duke of Grafton, I suppose, very frequently. The reports are so different, that I really cannot tell what to make of them. My Ld. Rockingham always insists that there is no alteration with regard to me; and Mr. Pitt still perseveres in his declaration that he will not act or sit in Council with me. Others seem to make more favourable representations; but I will suppose my Lord Rockingham to be in the right.

If I don't know exactly how things stand with Mr. Pitt, I as little know what the intentions of these Ministers are with regard to him, how far they will or will not comply with his conditions and what part they will act towards me.

I have had frequent conversations with my Lord Rockingham with regard to myself. He is always very civil, but says nothing explicite [sic] either about *him*self or *me*. Many of my friends have talked to him; they all seem to think he will not stay if I do not, but I believe they have only conjecture for it.

To me His Lordship seems to wish to have other reasons, besides what relate to me for quitting his employment. He supposes Mr. Pitt will make other conditions with regard to the party, and propose to remove some who are now in employments, to bring in his own friends. This I suppose His Lordship thinks will justify his quitting, to those who are so earnest for taking in Mr. Pitt, at any rate. Those I am afraid are some young relations, and, as I thought, friends of mine.

I have pressed my Lord Rockingham to bring things to a point, to know what Mr. Pitt will do, and then to determine what part he will take himself. His idea when I saw him last seem'd to be to bring Mr. Pitt in, as first or sole Minister to the King, not to remain in office himself but to insist with all his friends to remain in office, and to support Mr. Pitt, as he (Ld. Rockingham) declares he will do to the utmost of his power. By this means Lord Rockingham thinks *he* shall keep *the Whig party* together, and I suppose be himself at the head of it.

This scheme seems to me not very practicable, but till something is determined I shall avoid giving my opinion upon any thing. The King, who continues to be very gracious to me, assured me some days ago that none of his Ministers had said any thing to him of Mr. Pitt's coming into his service, ever since my Lord Rockingham sent the King's last answer to Mr. Pitt. And my Lord Rockingham told me the other day that he had not spoke to the King about it, and did not intend to do it, till something more certain was known of Mr. Pitt's intentions than there was at present.

For my own part whenever any resolution is taken, however unjustly I may be treated by Mr. Pitt or unkindly by my friends, if His Majesty and his present Ministers shall be of opinion that Mr. Pitt should be taken in, and that they can form an administration with him which may do the King's business and that of the publick, I shall adhere to the general contents of the paper deliver'd to the King, Jan^{ry} 8th last; and not be the sole obstacle to deprive the King and the publick of Mr. Pitt's service.

I have now finished the state of things as they appear to me to be, on this day, April the first, 1766; I pray God that the day may not be ominous.

HOLLES NEWCASTLE.

Claremont: *April* 1, 1766.

VIII

Fo. 52 b. Newcastle House : May 3,[1] 1766.

DEAR SIR,—With the same confidence and in the same expectation of knowing your thoughts and opinion upon our present situation I shall now acquaint you with the substance of what has passed since you left London, which will be a continuance of my former letters or narratives, the last of which was dated Claremont April 1st.

On Friday and Saturday last, Mr. Conway and the Duke of Grafton came to town; they were both with the King on Monday, and, as soon as they came out, the Duke of Grafton desired to speak to me, and Mr. Conway was present.

His Grace then told me, that he had acquainted the King that he hoped His Majesty would give him leave to resign his office, (I suppose as Mr. Pitt did not come into the King's service,) and he thought it a right attention to me to acquaint me with it.

You may imagine I expressed my concern at it, but to no purpose; His Grace was determined, tho' no particular time or rather day was then fixed. General Conway lamented it extremely, but was himself very willing and ready to go on, upon a proper plan of administration to be agreed amongst us. Mr. Conway declared his intention to see Mr. Pitt, and the Duke of Grafton and General Conway were together with Mr. Pitt on Tuesday night last, which put an end to any farther negotiation.

I attended His Majesty on Monday, when, as well as in the audiences I have had the honor to have since, the King was extremely gracious to me. His Majesty was pleased to acquaint me with what the Duke of Grafton had said to him, his endeavours to dissuade the Duke of Grafton from taking that

[1] Saturday.

part, but to no purpose ; and His Majesty's satisfaction to find that Mr. Conway would continue in his employment. The King order'd us, viz. my Lord Chancellor, my Lord Winchelsea, the Marquess of Rockingham, my Lord Egmont, Mr. Conway, and myself, to meet forthwith, and to give him our advice and opinion what to do, what measures to take and how to supply the Duke of Grafton's place.

His Majesty was pleased to give me a very particular account of what had passed with Mr. Conway and Mr. Pitt,[1] for His Majesty said he had had no report from the Duke of Grafton.

Mr. Pitt, I think, began by observing that he saw no possibility at present of his coming into the King's service, that in his opinion there must be a total change, or new disposition of the administration, that if he had any thing to do, he should be against all distinctions, parties or connections, that he would take the best and ablest men from them all. And I have also heard that he said, if he should incline to any line, it would be to that of the administration : but that he beg'd not great stress might even be laid upon that, that he would not open himself to anybody but to the King, and that I understand put an end to the whole.

Mr. Conway said he was extremely sorry for it and thought that Mr. Pitt was very much to blame in insisting to see the King, before His Majesty could have the least knowledge of what he intended to do, or to propose to the King.

Every thing passed very civilly on both sides, and Mr. Pitt talked of going soon to the Bath. He was in the House, the day the business of the Resolutions upon the American trade and the Address about the Free Port,[2] were to have been proposed. Mr. Alderman Beckford [3] moved to have this whole consideration put off for two months.

---

[1] Cf. on Pitt's conduct *Walpole* (Barker), ii. 223 *sqq*.
[2] Cf. *Walpole* (Barker), ii. 225.
[3] William Beckford, M.P. for London, Pitt's intimate friend. See *Lecky*, iii. 116.

Mr. Pitt opposed that notion strongly and said, tho' he differ'd at present about the Free Port, there were a great many very considerable men for it, that it was a question of great importance, that it might be right, and therefore that it ought to be thoroughly weigh'd and consider'd, and both parties should be heard, and that therefore he moved that the farther consideration should be put off to Monday only, the 5th instant, and that he thought the whole should be gone thro' now, and the point of the Free Port be now determined without any Address for a report from the Board of Trade upon it.

It is natural to suppose that he meant to be present himself on Monday, but it is said that he explained himself otherwise in private, but I suppose it is very uncertain whether he will be there or not.

The King told me on Monday with some little *observation*, that the Duke of Grafton had declared, the Monday before he went to Newmarket, to my Lord Rockingham and my Lord Albemarle that His Grace was determined to quit his employment, and, said the King, *I knew not one word of it till this morning.*

A little incident had happen'd on Tuesday which had put my Lord Chancellor out of humour. My Lord Rockingham proposed to the Chancellor to exchange his office, to be President of the Council as Lord Winchelsea was ready to resign it, and that Mr. Yorke should be made Chancellor. His Lordship flew into a violent passion, thought himself extremely ill-used, went and complained to the King, and refused either to have the meeting at his house, or to assist at a meeting with those who had used him so ill. His Majesty endeavoured to calm the Chancellor, and Lord Rockingham assured him that he thought the proposal would be agreeable to him or he would not have made it. Upon that the Chancellor came into temper, and our meeting was at his Lordship's house on Thursday last in the evening.

I believe my Lord Rockingham's real motive was one or both of these two. His Lordship knew I had mentioned my Lord Hardwicke as the most proper person to succeed the Duke of Grafton, and as my Lord Rockingham was, and, I suppose, is still for the Duke of Richmond, (and His Lordship and the Cavendishes are the only persons in the King's service who are of that opinion,) my Lord Rockingham might think it was necessary to him to satisfy *the Yorkes* another way, by making Mr. Charles Yorke Chancellor immediately.

The other motive was, (and that indeed I had from himself,) that the Duke of Richmond would make a very good Secretary [of] State when Mr. Yorke was Chancellor, and would be his (the Duke of Richmond's) governor. My Lord Rockingham might have thought of one who might be as proper a governor for the Duke of Richmond, who had been at the head of affairs, and of the House of Lords, for many years.[1] But those thoughts never come into his Lordship's head. Mr. Yorke is not yet a member of the House of Lords. Had my Lord Rockingham mentioned any thing of that kind to me, *I should not have undertaken the task*.

I shall now give you a particular account of what passed at our meeting at the Chancellor's on Thursday night last,[2] where were present Lord Chancellor, Lord Winchelsea, Marq of Rockingham, Earl of Egmont, Gen¹ Conway, and myself.

My Lord Chancellor made a long discontented speech; that he knew very little of the state of the administration, their connections, their views, &c.; and therefore could give no opinion or advice either for their continuing in their employments or for the supplying the Duke of Grafton's office of Secretary of State, as he did not know who would be agreable to the administration; that when the Ministry was formed, he believed he should, as he had always done, support His Majesty's administration.

[1] The Duke of Newcastle.
[2] May 1. On this meeting see *Walpole* (Barker), ii. 228, 229.

Mr. Conway then very properly open'd the affair,—that he thought if we could be sure of the concurrence and assistance of all those Lords and gentlemen of the House of Commons who are in His Majesty's service, a scheme might be formed for carrying on the administration with success, that in consideration of the indignity offer'd to the King in obliging His Majesty to dismiss Mr. Mackenzie in the manner that was done, Mr. Conway thought we might promise Mr. Mackenzie should have the first proper employment that might become vacant.

To this my Lord Rockingham and my Lord Winchelsea agreed, and they all declared they would go no further in satisfying Lord Bute's friends, except the keeping them in their places if they acted with and in support of the administration.

As to the keeping them in their places I entirely concur'd on condition that they acted thoroughly with us. I had my doubts about giving this assurance to Mr. Mackenzie and as I told the King, I should think it sufficient without making *any* previous *bargain* that His Majesty should understand that his Ministers did agree or would not object to His Majesty's giving a proper employment to Mr. Mackenzie when such a one should become vacant, and I believe that will satisfy the King on that head.

We, (that is, us four,) were all against treating with those gentlemen in a body but as particular persons possessed of great employments.

My Lord Egmont spoke long and often, and appear'd rather as counsel for my Lord Bute's friends. His Lordship said, that if we would go no farther than Mr. Conway proposed, that *that* would not do, that they (my Lord Bute's friends) were a body, that they must be treated with as such, that they would all act together as such, and the bare providing for Mr. Mackenzie was not sufficient, that they must be received with cordiality, that their friends must be consider'd in their turn and according to their merits, and seem'd to insinuate that some regard would be expected to be shew'd, and I think immediately, to my Ld. Northumberland, and Sir Fletcher Norton.

My Lord Egmont said that he had never consider'd them as a body till this winter, and then hinted at his conversation with Mr. Mackenzie. Lord Chancellor said that he had never look'd upon them as such till Sir Fletcher Norton had told him so in October last, with which his Lordship had acquainted the King at that time.

This conversation greatly alarmed us all, and alter'd much the nature of the consideration; if those gentlemen were to be treated with as a body to come in perhaps upon equal terms, it was impossible for us to agree to it. Lord Rockingham, Mr. Conway, my Lord Winchelsea, and myself were so strongly of that opinion that we look'd upon the whole affair as over. And thus the meeting broke up, Lord Rockingham and us three agreeing that nothing was to be done, and my Lord Rockingham particularly thinking that we had nothing further to do, and, for one, I apprehended that in a very short time we were to leave the King's service.

Thinking very naturally of the consequences of such a resolution if carried immediately into execution, I thought it my duty to write the enclosed letter[1] to my Lord Rockingham and to send a copy of it to Gen¹ Conway, who, with my Lord Winchelsea to whom he communicated it, and afterwards my Lord Rockingham, so much approved of it that I think this letter is the plan we are now going upon.

My Lord Egmont was a considerable time with the King, on Friday morning, before any of us saw His Majesty. Mr. Conway, Lord Rockingham and myself afterwards had our audiences, and all of us gave pretty near the same account to the King of what had passed the night before, at my Lord Chancellor's.

I was very full and particular in acquainting His Majesty

[1] Appendix (lost).

with every circumstance that had passed. His Majesty told us little of what my Lord Egmont had said, but order'd my Lord Rockingham to go to His Lordship to know what he knew of the sentiments or intentions of the party (Lord Bute's friends) for he had said nothing of them to the King, and that His Majesty knew very little about it, but drop'd to me, *that he knew my Lord Bute would not disturb his affairs*, or give any disturbance to his administration.

After having given the King a minute account of what had passed the night before, I took the liberty to talk very plainly to His Majesty: I asked him whether His Majesty wished the continuance of this administration? He said, *Yes*, certainly, but he did not like to be suspected; but seem'd to apply that more to what my Lord Rockingham had said than to what I was then saying.

I presumed also to ask His Majesty whether there was any person he could wish to have taken in? The King said, the case of my Lord Northumberland was very hard, that my Lord Northumberland was actually turned out by the last Ministry and was instrumental in bringing in this, and that no satisfaction was made him; that the Duke of Cumberland always said his case was hard, and that my Lord Rockingham had once *admitted* that it was; but that the circumstances of the times would not permit it to be done. I then said *and that is the case at present*.

His Majesty said no more, and I should fancy if other things were agreed, my Lord Northumberland would not finally be insisted upon. I spoke very plainly against all previous bargains, as well in the case of Mr. Mackenzie as of all the others.

And there the King left it; and refer'd to the explanation Lord Egmont would give to my Lord Rockingham, relating to that party.

I might do wrong, but at last I shew'd the King my letter

to my Lord Rockingham which goes enclosed ;[1] I am sure it had a good effect ; His Majesty read it over very carefully, and said *if anything could increase my regard for you it would be this letter.*

Thus things ended at Court on Friday last, and as I have as yet heard nothing from my Lord Rockingham of what passed with my Lord Egmont, I conclude there was nothing material.

IX

Fo. 59. Newcastle House: May 6, 1766, Tuesday.

I have the pleasure to acquaint you that on my return to town yesterday morning I found things much clear'd up and going on much better than I could have expected.

Lord Rockingham and Mr. Conway had both seen the King on Sunday, and had receiv'd His Majesty's orders, (agreably to what I had proposed) to sound the Lords and gentlemen of the House of Commons, who are under a certain description, as to the part they would take.

Lord Rockingham had a conversation yesterday in consequence of it with Mr. Elliot, which ended to my Lord Rockingham's satisfaction. Mr. Elliot said that my Lord Bute had discharged him, and gave him leave to do what was most agreable to himself, which plainly appeared to be to support the administration. I daresay the answer from them all will be the same.

Lord Talbot and Lord Litchfield have both assured His Majesty that they have no attachment but to the King, and are very ready to obey His Majesty's commands.

Lord Egmont has told the King that he has given his advice to us, to widen our bottom and to take in more of Lord Bute's friends, but if the Ministers did not think proper to follow his

[1] Not found.

advice, he should continue to act with them and support them as he has hitherto done.

Thus I think this affair will end, without any direct bargain or stipulation. *They* will see the King is in earnest to support his administration, and consequently they will do it, and by their doing it the world will think and see *that the King is in earnest*, as both Lord Rockingham and I verily believe he is.

I must now (and I rejoice to do it,) do justice to my Lord Rockingham's wise and steddy way of acting ever since our meeting at my Lord Chancellor's, on Thursday night last, and I cannot but be vain enough to think my letter on Friday morning has had some effect.

No man could have talked better, more wisely or stronger than he did both Sunday and Monday to the King; he has held the same language and I think better and more to the purpose than ever I have done myself, of the impossibility of our coming in or remaining in office upon any other foot than that of our declaration (with regard to my Lord Bute &c.) when we first came in, and the assurances the Duke of Cumberland gave us that all those gentlemen should join and support His Majesty's administration, which they had not yet done. His Majesty admitted the truth of that, and seem'd not displeased with my Lord Rockingham for having remember'd it.

The King was very gracious to me yesterday, who talked to him very honestly and very plainly. The whole now I think depends upon the choice of a proper Secretary of State. Lord Rockingham was to sound Lord Hardwicke,[1] last night, (I am sure that is the best). I don't know what has passed. I flung out a hasty notion to Mr. Conway, which he tastes very much. If Lord Hardwicke would not accept, why might not Charles Townshend be made a Peer and Secretary of State? But the

---

[1] Albemarle's *Rockingham*, i. 334 *sqq*. 'As poor a choice as could have been made' (*Walpole* [Barker], ii. 230).

best of all is the plan in my letter to my Lord Rockingham this morning, a copy of which is enclosed.[1]

This letter will be sent safe to you by Mr. Potts of the Post Office, and I desire you would enclose your answer to him in the same manner. I am, &c.,

HOLLES NEWCASTLE.

X

Fo. 60 b. Claremont : May 24, 1766.

Substance of what passed with the King on Thursday last, the 22nd instant.

As soon as I came into the King's Closet, His Majesty said, 'I have done all I could to avoid this,' meaning the appointment of the Duke of Richmond to be Secretary of State ; 'but I could not ;[2] I pressed my Lord Hardwicke to take the Seals, but he would not on any account. I afterwards would have had Charles Yorke take them, but he refused.[3] I don't think Mr. Yorke would have been farther from the Great Seal from being Secretary of State,' in which I perfectly agreed with His Majesty. ' But,' said the King, ' I found on Friday last, my Lord Rockingham so set upon having the Duke of Richmond that I did not know how to avoid it or what might have been the consequence.' (N.B.—I am not certain as to the words underlined but very certain as to the sense.) 'I asked my Lord Rockingham whether he could not find out somebody else ; he said he could not, and asked me (said the King) whether I could or not ? I told him, no, I knew of nobody, and so I did it. I know it will not do.' I replied, Your Majesty could do no more.

---

[1] A reference to the lost Appendix.

[2] The Duke was ' sensible how little he had been His Majesty's choice ' (*Walpole* [Barker], ii. 230). For Walpole's view of the appointment see *Letters*, iv. 500.

[3] *Vide* App. ' My letter to my Lord Rockingham, giving an account of my conversation with Mr. Charles Yorke.'

And here it may be proper to insert that the other day His Majesty who has never once failed to express his own disapprobation of the Duke of Richmond, and to mention several objections in which I never once concur'd, (having *singly* confined my reasons to the want of that experience which is necessary for that station in the present circumstances) press'd me to name some other person whom I might think more proper. I constantly declined it. At last His Majesty to shew how much he was in earnest, was pleased to ask me, ' Is there not a friend of your's, who has now another employment,' (meaning I am sure my Lord Grantham,) 'that would do?'

I at once foresaw the consequence of giving in to that proposal, and answer'd, Sir, no man in England would do the business of the office better, but he is not enough used to Parliamentary proceedings and conducting debates, and therefore I should rather think that in that respect he would not answer the purpose at present.

I foresaw that if I had given in to that measure, it would not only be taken extremely ill by my Lord Rockingham and Mr. Conway, and perhaps might occasion a total dissolution of this administration, but that that which had been so universally reported and adopted by Mr. Pitt, tho' without the least foundation, that the Duke of Newcastle had the direction of every thing, might, if Lord Grantham had been Secretary of State, have been believed with some colour of foundation : tho' I do verily believe that if I had concur'd in the King's own idea, His Majesty would have appointed my Lord Grantham. But to return to what passed in the closet on Thursday last.

The King was pleased in talking of the Duke of Richmond's inexperience in the House of Lords to say, ' He must be under direction, he must have *a governor*.' To which I replied, But who, Sir, can be that Governor? 'Why not yourself?'

I answer'd that I hoped His Majesty would excuse my undertaking any such thing, that I had declined every thing of that sort.

His Majesty often mentioned the Duke of Richmond's temper, and that he would not agree with the other Ministers. In that I beg'd leave to differ with His Majesty, for that I did believe the Duke of Richmond was a man of honor, and that he had such obligation to my Lord Rockingham and Genl Conway, that he would not differ with them.

I then took the liberty to enter fully into my own situation; that I had given my opinion according to my conscience upon the point, which His Majesty had refer'd to me and the rest of his servants, relating to the person the most proper to succeed to the Duke of Grafton. I had been of opinion first for Lord Hardwicke, then for my Lord Egmont,[1] but that I could not concur in advising the Duke of Richmond on account of his youth and want of sufficient experience; that I did it from no sort of prejudice to the Duke of Richmond or want of real regard and attention to His Grace. This it was necessary to say, as the King had told me that Lord Rockingham said that my objection to the Duke of Richmond, he believed, arose from our disputes in Sussex,[2] which had lower'd the Duke of Richmond in my opinion. The King was pleased to take it up very warmly and said to my Lord Rockingham, 'My Lord, how can you think that one of the Duke of Newcastle's age, and (I think, His Majesty added) experience, can be jealous of a boy?'

I could not forbear representing to His Majesty, the little regard and confidence which had been shew'd to me, of which His Majesty himself had often express'd his strong disapprobation; that I should continue, as I had done, to support

---

[1] In the margin the Duke adds: 'I am not positive that I mentioned this of my Ld. Hardwicke and my Ld. Egmont to the King at that time.'

[2] Where the Duke was Lord Lieutenant.

His Majesty's affairs, that I did not mean to quit my employment, but that if I found the same *backwardness*, reserve, want of communication and confidence, to continue, I hoped His Majesty would allow me to withdraw from the private meetings of his Ministers, where my presence in those circumstances could be of no service to His Majesty and the publick and must be so disagreable to myself.

His Majesty was pleased to answer me in the most gracious manner, to approve what I had said and the manner in which I so properly supported *my own honor and dignity*. And as a proof that I shall act according to what I have declared to the King, I attended my Lord Rockingham, Mr. Conway, and Mr. Dowdeswell all day and night on Thursday, and shall meet them at my Lord Chancellor's on Monday evening.

My Lord North having finally refused the Vice Treasurer's [1] place, a good deal of discourse passed upon the persons most proper to have the offer of it. It was generally agreed that Mr. Stanley [2] might be sounded, but from what I have since heard I do not believe that there is the least likelyhood that Mr. Stanley would accept it.

It was understood that my Lord Dartmouth should have the whole correspondence with America, whether as third Secretary of State or as First Lord of Trade with the power of Secretary of State, was not, I think, determined.

I had forgot one pretty extraordinary circumstance in my conversation with the King.

In talking to His Majesty of my Lord Rockingham's coolness to me and little inclination to consult me, or even to have any assistance from me, I mentioned a late incident, that in coming the other day out of His Majesty's closet, I found Lord Rockingham and Lord Egmont sitting together; I began by blaming my Lord Egmont for not accepting the Seals; my

---

[1] Of Ireland. Cf. *Grenville Correspondence*, iii. 239.
[2] Hans Stanley. See *Grenville* and *Chatham Correspondence*.

Lord Egmont said to me, Why don't you take them yourself? That will remove all difficulties.[1] I said that was impossible, that, to remove every possibility of that kind I had declared publickly in the House of Lords that I would not ever accept any Ministerial office of that sort. And I told the King that my Lord Rockingham said not one word upon it, or made me the least compliment, which His Lordship might have done very safely. Yes, said the King, I know it. Lord Egmont told me of it, and was much surprized at my Lord Rockingham's silence.

I add here copies of my letter to the Duke of Richmond, His Grace's answer and my answer to him.[2] I shall shew them to the King and I am persuaded His Majesty will be very well pleased with the Duke of Richmond's letter, and that it will be of service to His Grace with the King.

XI.

Fo. 64 b.   Newcastle House: June 28, 1766, Saturday morning.

Some occurrences of yesterday sent to Mr. White.

My Lord Albemarle came to see me yesterday morning, at Mr. Onslow's,[3] and acquainted me that my Lord Rockingham had received the King's orders, on Wensday last, for appointing the Duke of York[4] warden of Windsor Forest, which is supposed to give the influence over Windsor Town; and also to appoint His Royal Highness Ranger of Cranborn Chace &c., and to appoint His Royal Highness, Prince Henry,[5] who has Beaumont Lodge, in the neighbourhood, Ranger of Windsor Park. That His Royal Highness the Duke of Gloucester[6] had got Gen¹ Pulteney's regiment, and Col. West was made Aid de-camp: and that all these appointments were made without any com-

[1] No doubt said satirically.
[2] A reference to the Appendix.
[3] The Duke of Newcastle's nephew.
[4] Edward Augustus, the King's brother.
[5] Henry Frederick, another brother.
[6] William Henry, another brother.

munication with, or the knowledge of, any of the Ministry.[1] My Lord Albemarle seemed very much affected with it; and said, that, as to himself, he had done at court; that he should come seldom thither; that he had no pretence to come into the inward rooms, having now nothing to say to the King in the closet. I asked my Lord Albemarle what my Lord Rockingham had said to him *upon this*? He said *nothing*. He told me a pretty extraordinary conversation which his good brother, the Admiral,[2] had had with my Lord Talbot, which perhaps may give some key to what has been lately doing at S. James's, and to His Lordship's last speech in the House of Lords.

My Lord Talbot, it seems, pretends now to be in love with the Duke of Grafton. He said to Admiral Keppel: Your brother (my Lord Albemarle) is entirely attached to my Lord Rockingham and the Duke of Newcastle, but *you* cannot be against Mr. Pitt. The Admiral replied, I? No; I have always been one of Mr. Pitt's best friends.

My Lord Talbot has had many long audiences of the King of late. My Lord Talbot to be sure, perhaps my Lord Egmont also, has negotiated these distinctions which are now shewn to the young princes. I am persuaded that this whole affair, and the present coolness of the closet, are entirely owing to the unfortunate step of promising the King to bring the provision, proposed for the princes' establishment, into parliament, this winter, and afterwards not doing it, which has been worked up by the Princess Dowager of Wales.

I went, according to appointment, to Gen¹ Conway's; and I found that it was to be a meeting of consequence indeed. Lord Rockingham did not come till after one o'clock, so we had not much time for such a material deliberation. I found the business was, to consider what it might be proper for us to say to the King, upon the present state of the administration.

---

[1] On the discussion concerning the provision for the King's brothers see *Walpole* (Barker), ii. 233.   [2] Lord Albemarle's brother, Admiral Keppel.

It was proposed by them three, that we should all lay before the King the necessity of His Majesty's giving some publick demonstration of his resolution to support his present administration. That this should be introduced by, and chiefly founded upon, an intercepted letter from M. Gross, nephew of the late M. Gross, Minister here from the Empress of Russia; wherein this M. Gross advises Her Imperial Majesty not to conclude, at present, the treaty now depending with Russia; as it is generally thought that the present administration cannot last long, as they have not the confidence of the King, their master.

This was thought, as it certainly is, a very proper foundation to speak to the King upon, and to insist with His Majesty that some demonstration should be given by him to contradict these reports, or otherwise his affairs, both at home and abroad, must suffer; and particularly that that demonstration should be given by immediately removing Mr. Dyson [1] and my Lord Eglintoun.[2]

It was also proposed, chiefly by the Duke of Richmond, that in case His Majesty should not agree to what should be thus proposed to him, that the administration should declare that they could no longer continue in his service.

To the first part I entirely agreed—viz. the necessity of His Majesty giving some demonstration of his resolution to support the present administration, founded upon appearances and particularly upon the intercepted letter above mentioned:[3] but I was of opinion, that the threatening the King to leave his service, in case His Majesty should not comply with what should be proposed to him that morning, was an affair of too much consequence to be determined in half an hour, and by us four only.

---

[1] Jeremiah Dyson, M.P. for Great Yarmouth. On him see *Walpole* (Barker), ii. 235, 236; *Chatham Correspondence*, ii. 394; and Albemarle's *Rockingham*, i. 306, 346.

[2] Lord of the Bedchamber. *Grenville Correspondence*, iii. 254. Both he and Dyson were King's Friends, and in Bute's confidence. On the question of his removal see *Walpole* (Barker), ii. 236; *Bedford Correspondence*, iii. 338.

[3] Cf. *Rockingham*, i. 322.

Accordingly we all went to court to execute the first part of the proposal. It was agreed that the two Secretaries of State should go in first. Afterwards my Lord Rockingham; and myself, the last. Accordingly the two Secretaries went in first, and stayed a great while with the King.

When they came out, Lord Rockingham went in. His Lordship did not stay with the King above five minutes. The Secretaries, I believe, enter'd very fully with the King into the matter. His Majesty was very civil; but, to us all, very negative. He wondered that the Secretaries should lay such a stress upon a silly letter from M. Gross; that, as to reports, which there was no foundation for, no regard ought to be had to them. That he was very well satisfied with his administration; that he intended to support them, and to remove those who should act against them *for the future*: but that he could not have any regard to what was past; that Mr. Dyson acted like an honest man, in telling my Lord Rockingham his opinion; that he thought the measures which had been taken were wrong: but that if Mr. Dyson should, in the course of the summer, obstruct the measures of the administration at the Board of Trade, or vote against them next winter in parliament, he would then turn him out.

His Majesty said but little about Lord Eglintoun; but was disposed to remove him, but said particularly, as to Mr. Dyson's behaviour in the question about the provision for the princes, that as that affair related to the King himself, he would not turn him out for that.

My Lord Rockingham stayed but a very little while; he talked in the same manner the Secretaries had done, and received the same answers, and that was pretty near my case.

His Majesty began with me by acquainting me with the difference of opinion between his three Ministers; that my Lord Rockingham had recommended to him two months ago, General Honeywood for the government of Hull, when it should be vacant; that tho' he had not given my Lord Rockingham an absolute promise, yet he had said enough to my Lord Rockingham to give great encouragement to General Honeywood to hope for it. That now the Duke of Argyle put in for it, and said he would quit the service if he had not the government of Hull. That Mr. Conway and the Duke of Richmond were both for the Duke of Argyle.

His Majesty seemed strongly on the side of my Lord Rockingham, and, indeed, I encouraged His Majesty in it. The King was mightily pleased with my Lord Granby, who had been with him, and told him, that he would not recommend his uncle, my Lord Robert Manners, who was Lieutenant-Governor of Hull to be Governor, because he would not lay His Majesty under any difficulty. His Majesty hopes that General Conway will be able to persuade the Duke of Argyle to desist.

I then acquainted the King, that I understood his Ministers had laid before His Majesty the state of the administration, that I entirely concur'd with them, that it was necessary for His Majesty's service, that some demonstration should be given of His Majesty's resolution to support his present administration, to contradict these reports, and to prevent the ill-effects of these advices from Foreign Ministers.

His Majesty treated it in the same manner that he had done with the other Ministers. I stuck a little closer, and as I had a precedent in point, I made the best use of it I could. I told the King that I remembered very well, that, in Sir Robert Walpole's administration, Count Staremberg, the Emperor's Minister, and M. Chavigny, the French Minister, were in close correspondence with my Lord Granville, Sir William Wyndham, and Mr. Pulteney,[1] then in Opposition, that we intercepted all their letters, and saw all that had passed between them, and the opposers; that there were frequent suggestions, in their letters,

---

[1] Cf. Hervey's *Memoirs of George II.* ii. 250, on the interception of these letters.

that Sir R. Walpole had not the King's affection, but that His Majesty was, in his heart, disposed to my Lord Granville; that Sir Robert Walpole had constantly made the same use of those letters, with the late King, as His Majesty's Ministers had now done of this letter from M. Gross with His Majesty; viz. to show the necessity that some demonstration should be given, by the King, to prove the contrary.

His Majesty made little or no reply to this. I enter'd particularly into the case of Mr. Dyson, but to no effect.

Upon the whole the King was very civil to me. But I could plainly discover, that His Majesty was not pleased with my entering so far into this matter; which I thought myself both in conscience and duty bound to do.

What will be the end of all this, I know not; I think the Duke of Richmond and Mr. Conway will insist upon some further éclaircissements with the King. What my Lord Rockingham will do, I know not. I take His Lordship's view to be different from the other two. My Lord Rockingham, I believe, wishes to go out, and flatters himself, that he shall go out with more éclat than any man ever did; that he has done great service to the King, and to the publick; that he had shew'd the King that he could carry the repeal of the Stamp Act, with His Majesty, and my Lord Bute[1] against him; that he could carry the Free Port with Mr. Pitt against him; and had carried all the regulations, that were proper, relating to the American trade.

I could add to this, that, if His Lordship had thought proper to have taken my advice in the beginning, for the total Repeal of the Stamp Act, and had not amused himself, and flattered others, with senseless notion of *modification*, of which the King availed himself in his discourse with me upon that point, His Lordship had deprived Mr. Pitt of the opportunity that was given him, to

---

[1] *Walpole* (Barker), ii. 211, on the 'childish arrogance and indiscretion' of Lord Rockingham's vaunt.

take almost the whole merit, both at home, and in America, of the Repeal of that Act.

My Lord Rockingham dropt, at our meeting, that, if there could be any way of getting the Duke of Bedford, and his friends, without Mr. Grenville,[1] he thought that would be the best acquisition we could make. Mr. Conway replied, in that case there must be great removes amongst our own friends to make way for them. I must do them all three the justice to say, that I did not see the least inclination in any one of them, to have any management for, or correspondence with, my Lord Bute or any of his friends.

My Lord Rockingham told me, in private, that Mr. Pitt would have nothing to do with this administration.

I should have observed, that it was suggested, that His Majesty might be asked what it was His Majesty wished, or expected, of his Ministers; but that, for very obvious reasons, was dropt.

It was, I think, agreed, that in order to please the King, it might be proposed to send Mr. Ellis,[2] ambassador to Spain, in the room of my Lord Rochford, who is appointed ambassador to France. That it was accordingly mentioned to the King; and is to be proposed to Mr. Ellis; I am sorry for it; he is not a very proper person, and the King seem'd very indifferent about it; but however it is to be.

By what my Lord Rockingham said to me yesterday, I find, it is his intention, before he goes, to oblige as many of our friends as he can; that is very proper, but it would have been more effectual, if the resolution had been taken sooner.

We had, last night, a meeting at my Lord Chancellor's, upon the instructions to be given to the new Governor of Canada,[3] and

[1] *Rockingham*, i. 349.
[2] Welbore Ellis; he did not become ambassador. Cf. Chesterfield's *Letters*, iii. 1342.
[3] Lieutenant-General Murray On the Canadian question see *Rockingham*, i. 351. 350, and *Chatham Correspondence*, ii. 434 *note*.

altho' they had passed the Council, and the opinion of the Attorney- and Solicitor-general was had upon them, and the draught was made in consequence by the Board of Trade, my Lord Chancellor said so much against the original principle of authorizing the Governor to constitute Courts of Justice &c., which power was given them by the original commission in the late Ministry's time ; and whether, without the consent of Parliament, His Majesty has it in his power, in any of his dominions, to appoint a Roman Catholick to be Justice of Peace &c., that nothing was determined, when I left them, last night : but I am apt to think, the instructions will go, as they are agreable, in the greatest part, to the opinion of the Attorney- and Solicitor-general. It is much to be lamented, that the Privy Council, where all these things are settled, has not the assistance of any one law lord, the Chancellor very seldom attending those Councils. My Lord Hardwicke takes a very active part at all our meetings.

I send this account to my friend Mr. White, to be added to those I formerly sent. I leave it open for the Duke of Portland's perusal ; and hope soon to have His Grace's thoughts, and Mr. White's, upon this paper.

XII

Fo. 71 b.   Claremont : July 11,[1] 1766.

DEAR SIR,—As I am desirous that you should be constantly informed of everything, as far, as it comes to my knowledge, relating to the situation of the administration, and of publick affairs, and of my own situation, in particular ; I must now acquaint you that my Lord Chancellor, (who you will have seen by my last account was very much dissatisfied with the administration, and indeed, he had shewed it, often, both at our meetings, and in private

---

[1] Cf. letters of this date from Walpole to Sir Horace Mann (iv.) ; and Lord Hardwicke to Lord Rockingham, in *Rockingham*, i. 363.

to me,) waited upon the King, last night, full of complaints and dissatisfaction. You will see the account of what passed in his audience in the copies of the two letters[1] I now send you, from the Duke of Richmond, and my Lord Rockingham.

I was sent for up to town by my Lord Rockingham, and the Duke of Richmond. The Duke of Richmond, my Lord Rockingham, my Lord Dartmouth, Gen¹ Conway and myself, met at Mr. Conway's house,[2] on Wensday morning last, and we there determined to wait upon the King, to learn His Majesty's thoughts and intentions; His Majesty having said to his Ministers, that he must consider, what was to be done; and whether this step of my Lord Chancellor had been concerted, or not, with His Majesty, or anybody else.

I found that it was my Lord Rockingham's opinion, that if this should appear to be no more than a flight in the Chancellor, and that the King would give the seals to Mr. Yorke, and make some proper removals to demonstrate his real intention to support the present administration, that everything might go on with ease and success; and that the additional strength of having Mr. Yorke Chancellor, and in the House of Lords, would make a very good alteration in favor of the present administration. We all went that day to court: but we soon found that the King had taken his part; so far, at least, as to send for Mr. Pitt; and from thence we supposed to form such an administration as Mr. Pitt should advise:—but what that administration was to be, or from whom this advice came, was not known to any of us, when I left my Lord Rockingham late on Wensday night last.

The Ministers think that they know that my Lord Bute saw the King at Richmond on Monday last; and that the Duke of York was sent for to come to town, (as he did) from Bath. This

---

[1] A reference to the Appendix. Cf. *Walpole* (Barker), ii. 237; Walpole's *Letters*, iv. 510, on the Chancellor, 'who can smell a storm and has probably bargained for beginning it.'   [2] July 9. See *Rockingham*, i. 362.

may be conjecture, but you will see the inference, that is drawn from it.

My Lord Rockingham went accordingly to the King *first*; and told His Majesty that, as he had been pleased to say, *he must consider what was to be done*, my Lord Rockingham desired to know His Majesty's thoughts. The King said, that upon consideration, *he had sent for Mr. Pitt.*[1] My Lord Rockingham neither made any objection, nor reason'd upon it: but hoped he had served His Majesty faithfully, and agreably to what he had declared to the King, upon his first coming into His Majesty's service, a year ago. He explained the several measures, which had been taken by His Majesty's Ministers this session of Parliament; and how they had all succeeded. And he had now the satisfaction to acquaint His Majesty, that, by the last accounts from America, the Repeal of the Stamp Act had had all the good effect, that could be proposed; had been received with the utmost duty, and gratitude; and that everything was quiet in America and no one mark left of disobedience, or discontent. The King replied he was perfectly satisfied with him.

The Secretaries were longer with His Majesty. The King expressed great satisfaction with Mr. Conway; and hoped that whatever administration he should have, he should have Mr. Conway's service; meaning in the place where he was. The King was very civil to them all, and said he was very well satisfied with their services.[2] As soon as I came into the closet, His Majesty gave me an account of what had passed with the Chancellor; and I found that what the Chancellor had said of the weakness, and insufficiency of this administration, had made an impression upon him, and I think His Majesty had a mind to

---

[1] *Chatham Correspondence*, ii. 434; Walpole, *Letters*, iv. 510; (Barker) ii. 239. On the negotiations with Pitt see also the 'History of the Late Minority' in Almon's *Political Register*, i. 312, also Almon's *Anecdotes of the Earl of Chatham*, ii. 21 *sqq.*

[2] Cf. *Walpole* (Barker), ii. 239, 240, who states that the King was harsh to Newcastle, and to Richmond not tolerably civil.

infer, from all we had said to him, of the necessity of his giving some demonstration of his intention, and inclination, to support his present administration, that *we ourselves* thought the administration weak. And the King then said, *I have sent for Mr Pitt*: but, said His Majesty, I know nothing more; I believe he will come; that was, to obey the King's orders, to come to him.—His Majesty enter'd into no particulars, talked very civilly of all his Ministers: but I see the intention is (that is, Mr. Pitt's intention) to keep Mr. Conway Secretary of State.

The King was very gracious to me; was pleased to say, no man in England had done so much service to his family as I had;—and, said His Majesty, from the year 1714.

Upon my making a proper reply, and expressing my desire since I last came in, to do everything in my power for his service, His Majesty said, Yes, you had done *great service* and *would have done more, if they would have let you, or trusted you*;—but whether service in general, or in particular, to the Ministers, I cannot say: for the King might very likely mean to the Ministers, as His Majesty had very often insinuated to me, the use I might be of to them, from my long experience, and knowledge of business; and his concern, that they did not consult me, so much as he thought they should do.

I have often observed in the King, some apprehension that the present administration wanted strength, experience, and precision in business: but I never imagined that His Majesty would have taken this step without consulting them, or previously informing them of it; especially as the King had so often declared that, after the advances he had made to Mr. Pitt, he would not send to him to come, before he knew what he would propose, or he had explained himself in general to his Ministers.

I do suppose that this sudden resolution must be taken in concert with my Lord Bute,[1] and consequently, the Princess

---

[1] *Grenville Correspondence*, iii. 262, and *Rockingham*, i. 367.

of Wales, and possibly the Duke of York. In all events, I should think, Mr. Pitt (if he engages, of which, I think, there is still a great doubt,) will form his plan upon the declaration he has made, 'To take the best men without distinction of parties or *connections*;' that he will propose to keep as many of the present Ministers, as he shall think will be attached to him ; and particularly the Duke of Grafton, and Gen¹ Conway ; and that he will offer others, who perhaps may not be disposed to remain in their employments. For my own part, I shall certainly not engage in a new administration, and I am persuaded Mr. Pitt will not make me the offer in any shape.

I have, upon this occasion, repeated my assurances of friendship and regard to my Lord Rockingham ; and I shall certainly make them good. I had very kind answers from His Lordship ; that he should be desirous to live in private friendship with me ; but that, as to publick affairs, he should act as he himself thought right for him to do, and, (as I understood) without any concert with anybody ; that he should neither persuade, nor dissuade, any one man in employment, to remain or go out : and yet he has sent expresses to the Duke of Portland, Sir George Savile, Lord Hardwicke, Lord Egmont &c. to come to town.

I could not avoid asking why he did that, if he did not intend to consult them, or to consider what we should do in the present circumstances. Don't fear me, I will do nothing wrong, either for myself, or the publick, for my friends, or the Whig cause.

I should be glad to have your advice as soon, and as fully, as you can give it me ; and you may send your letter by express enclosed to my trusty friend Mr. Potts, at the Post Office.

I had a letter from that honest man, my good friend Mr. Hewett.¹ I think he seems a little uneasy, I am sure he shall never have any reason to be so with me. I beg you would tell him so, and acquaint him with the contents of this letter, as far

¹ Probably the M.P. for Notts.

as relates to the sending for Mr. Pitt, and what had passed in the closet upon it.

I suppose you will not see our good, honest, and sensible friend, the Duke of Portland. He is now, I understand, at Chatsworth. I wrote him two lines by Lord Rockingham's messenger, to shew my regard to him; and that I was acquainted that my Lord Rockingham was sending a messenger to him. I believe he does not know the particulars I am sending you: but I hope you will take an early opportunity to acquaint him with them, as well as to send me your thoughts upon this late event, and upon what I sent you by the Duke of Portland.

Fo. 75 b.   Claremont: July 20, 1766.

As I found by the Duke of Portland that he had fully acquainted you with the substance of my letter of the 11th, I determined not to send it away, but to wait till I could give some account of Mr. Pitt's arrival, and of what should pass upon it.

Hitherto His Majesty has not been pleased to say anything more than that he had sent for Mr. Pitt, either to my Lord Rockingham, Gen¹ Conway, the Duke of Richmond or myself; nor has the King acquainted any of us that he had seen either Mr. Pitt, or my Lord Temple :—but I will give you some account of what has passed before the final resolution is taken, or any plan proposed or agreed to.

On Friday the 13th inst. Mr. Pitt arrived in town; and went, as is said, immediately to my Lord Chancellor, who has been the grand negotiator for settling an administration.

On Saturday Mr. Pitt was a great while with the King at Richmond, of which not one word transpires.

On Sunday last, Mr. Pitt had a long conversation with Mr. Conway, by his own appointment. Mr. Pitt was also that morning with my Lord Lincoln at the Exchequer. I have not heard one word of what passed there to this hour: but Mr. Pitt told Mr. Conway that he had been that morning with my Lord Lincoln.

Mr. Pitt did not say any thing to Mr. Conway of what had passed with the King; or give him any account of his being sent for, or coming to His Majesty; he talked as Minister, who was to settle every thing; which I suppose he concluded Mr Conway knew.[1]

He began by expressing his wishes, (which he had declared in publick,) that an administration could be formed of the best and ablest men,—without any regard to parties, distinctions, or *connections* : but as he despair'd of being able to bring that about, the Whig party must be the *basis* or *foundation*, and consequently the present administration; that he, Mr. Pitt, could wish to make no alterations at all; but that *that* was not to be avoided; that he had some friends that he must bring in; that he hoped that Mr. Conway had preserved the same good disposition towards him, (Mr. Pitt,) that he had when Mr. Pitt saw him last, or, I think the expression was, 'that Mr. Pitt had carried with him into the country;' and that therefore Mr. Pitt desired to have Mr. Conway's assistance for the conduct of the House of Commons; and I think as Secretary of State; that Mr. Pitt could not undertake the House of Commons himself; neither would he be *Secretary of State*.

Mr. Conway made a very proper answer which Mr. Pitt seemed to approve. Mr. Conway told him that Mr. Pitt knew how desirous he had been of acting with him, but that things were very much changed, since that time; that therefore Mr. Conway could not give any answer till he knew what was designed, the plan of administration, and the measures.

Mr. Pitt then proceeded and said he was much concerned; that he should think two things necessary, which he feared would not be agreable to Mr. Conway; the one, what related to the Duke of Richmond; the other, the necessity, he was

[1] Cf. *Walpole* (Barker), ii. 241 *sqq*.

under, of making an offer of the Treasury, to my Lord Temple. He said my Lord Temple was sent for not by him; but, insinuated, by the King, as he was; that is, by my good Lord Chancellor, the amanuensis of the whole.

He talked of my Lord Bute's friends, and (I think, as another point, that might not be agreable to Mr. Conway) Mr. Pitt said, he had no objection to restoring Mr. Stuart Mackenzie to his office of Privy Seal in Scotland;[1] or to my Lord Northumberland's having an office of distinction. This was the substance of that conversation.

Mr. Conway expressed to me his great conflict with himself upon the difficulties he was under. That he had lately suffered a great deal, from the dilemma he had been in, whether to leave the King's service, and his friends in the administration, to go out with the Duke of Grafton for the sake of Mr. Pitt; and that he had resolved to remain with the present Ministers. That the same difficulty now arose, tho' in another shape: viz. whether he should go out with the present Ministers, or remain with his friend the Duke of Grafton, upon Mr. Pitt's coming into the administration. He seemed to think that my Lord Temple being part of the new administration or not, might make a great difference in that question. He told me that the Duke of Grafton had a great dislike to my Lord Temple; that His Grace had declined coming to town; that he would not come to be jangling about the disposal of employments: but when Mr. Pitt sent for His Grace, he came to town immediately, I think, on Wensday last.

Mr. Conway told me the Duke of Grafton was now most strongly of opinion to come in, and support Mr. Pitt's administration; even tho' my Lord Temple should be a part of it. I found Mr. Conway under the same difficulties with regard to himself, as he was before.

The Duke of Portland, my Lord Albemarle, Lord John

---

[1] He was restored July 1766. See *Walpole* (Barker), ii. 25.

Cavendish and myself, dined with my Lord Rockingham, on Wensday last. We talked fully over the present situation. I mentioned Mr. Conway's difficulties, which my Lord Rockingham very properly admitted, as well as that we ought to speak our opinions freely to General Conway ; and my Lord Rockingham did very properly give his opinion as follows, that our utmost endeavours should be used to engage the Duke of Grafton and Mr. Pitt to consent that the Duke of Grafton should be at the head of the Treasury ; that *that* would be the only real security to the party ; (and to be sure, that is much to be wished ;) if my Lord Rockingham will not remain there himself, or they won't let him, as since appears to be the case : but that if neither the Duke of Grafton, nor any known friend, was to be at the head of the Treasury, and especially if Lord Temple was to come there, my Lord Rockingham thinks all hopes of saving the party, by this administration, were at an end. And that the only thing then to be wished was, that neither Mr. Conway nor any of our principal friends, should remain in the administration ; and that seemed to be the general opinion.

On Wensday, we all saw the King ; His Majesty was equally silent to us all, and to Mr. Conway, whom he intends to keep Secretary of State. I took a pretence to go into the closet to see whether the King, (when it came now so near, and was probably to begin by my removal) would mention any thing of it to me, to whom His Majesty had at times talked in confidence upon those subjects, and particularly with regard to his present ministers, and Mr. Pitt ;—but not one word ; very civil ; and full of discourse about my Lady Montrath's will.[1]

Upon this, I thought I had nothing to do but to return hither ; where I shall stay 'till Wensday next (my usual day of coming to town) ; if I am not sent for sooner. I did not go to court on Thursday but was engaged to dine at Gen¹ Conway's

---

[1] Cf. Walpole, *Letters*, v. 1, on Lady Mountrath's bequest to the Duchess of Newcastle.

with my Lord Rockingham, the Duke of Richmond, the Duke of Portland, &c.

I returned hither, in the evening, and at twelve o'clock, at night, had an account from my good friend, George Onslow, of my Lord Temple's resolution to return to Stowe, without accepting any employment;[1] of which I had from my friend Lord Rockingham the enclosed full account[2] early the next morning; which, least it should not be publick enough, is (I suppose by my Lord Temple's order) inserted, with the reasons, in all the newspapers. All our friends, and myself as much as any, were extremely pleased ; and hoped that great good would, and must, come from it.

You will see[2] my sense of it by my answer to my Lord Rockingham, and the letter I wrote to Gen¹ Conway. I am sorry to say that Gen¹ Conway's letter seems to suppose more difficulties than I at first apprehended. I shall do my part, however, in endeavouring to get over them.

There dined here this day the Duke of Richmond, the Duke of Portland, the Marquess of Rockingham, Earl of Albemarle, Earl Spencer, Visct. Villiers, Lord John Cavendish, Lord Grantham, Genl. Conway, Adml. Keppel, Sir Chas. Saunders, Sir George Savile, Mr. Dowdeswell, Sir Matthew Fetherstone, Mr. Chas. Townshend—Spanish,[3] Mr. Onslow, Duke of Newcastle. You may imagine that nothing passed as to the present situation of affairs in so large a company. I heard, however, that most of the company, in their little separate *coteries*, seemed strongly for going on with, and supporting Mr. Pitt's administration.

I had an opportunity of talking privately to some of them, particularly to my Lord Rockingham, the Duke of Richmond,

---

[1] *Grenville Correspondence*, iii. 266, 272 *sqq*.

[2] A reference to the Appendix.

[3] Not the celebrated Charles, but the son of Colonel W. Townshend. Called Spanish as secretary to the ambassador at Madrid (*Walpole* [Barker], ii. 134 *note*).

the Duke of Portland, and Mr. Conway; and I found some difference of opinion with regard to the part to be taken by our friends, and the support to be given to Mr. Pitt's administration. But as it was not at all then known what that administration was to be, no resolution was come to, except that my Lord Rockingham, and some others were to meet Mr. Conway the next morning; but I understand there was nothing more determined at that meeting. We were all to meet on Wensday the 23rd at court, when we concluded, (as was the case) we should be more fully informed of what was intended.

Fo. 80 b.   Claremont: July 25, 1766.

I shall now give you a full account of what passed at court on Wensday last[1]; and of the situation of things as they now stand, as far as is come to my knowledge.

We were all at court and were very civilly received at the levee. Mr. Pitt had been with the King two hours at the Queen's house, that morning. My Lord Chancellor went into the closet first, and stayed a great while there; but said not one word to anybody upon his coming out.

Mr. Conway told me, and I conclude my Lord Rockingham also, that we should hear from the King the dispositions that were intended; that he believed there would be no other alterations; and particularly told me that he thought it was not designed to remove the Duke of Portland.

The Duke of Richmond went in first, to whom His Majesty did not say one single word, relating to the administration, or to His Grace himself.

Mr. Conway went in next, alone, stayed a great while with the King; and confirmed what he had said to me before.

My Lord Rockingham went next, stayed a great while with His Majesty, but gave me no further account of what had passed,

[1] July 23.

than that the King had acquainted him with the design'd alterations; and had expressed himself in the most gracious manner imaginable to His Lordship.

The Lord of the Bedchamber had acquainted the King from the beginning with my being there, and with my desire to have an audience of His Majesty. The King order'd him to send the Duke of Grafton in; (who, I understand, had been sent for;) His Grace stayed with His Majesty so long, that it was five o'clock before I could get admittance. And I will now acquaint you with every circumstance that passed, as far as my memory will serve me; as I am desirous every true friend of mine should be informed of it.

When I came into the King's closet, at five o'clock, His Majesty said: as I know how well my Lord Rockingham and you wish me, I will acquaint you with all that has passed, as I have my Lord Rockingham; and then the King proceeded.

After it was over with my Lord Temple, (of which His Majesty did not give me any account, tho' he would tell me every thing) the following arrangement has been agreed to; the Duke of Grafton to succeed my Lord Rockingham as First Lord of the Treasury. I think the King said he was sorry for my Lord Rockingham: but I am sure His Majesty said, I love my Lord Rockingham: and am ready to give him any *other* employment now, or whenever he shall desire to have *any other* employment.

I told His Majesty that since my Lord Rockingham was not to remain, I was very glad the Duke of Grafton was to succeed him. That His Majesty knew how sincerely I had wished, that he might have Mr. Pitt's service: but it was *in conjunction with his present Ministers*; that I had often told the King that the present Ministers executed their offices, and particularly my Lord Rockingham, extremely well. His Majesty admitted that I had done so.) I added that they had gained great credit in the nation, and particularly in the City, by their conduct and measures in parliament. And that I was persuaded that Mr. Pitt would not increase his popularity by removing them, and also that if Mr. Pitt's principles were, (as I believed they were) such as he had professed ; and that he would act up to them, I did not think that he could find any one set of men in this kingdom, that would enable him so to do, and to serve His Majesty upon that foot so well, as His Majesty's present Ministers. The King made no reply but looked civil.

The King then said smilingly, You know *he will have your employment.* I answer'd, And I am ready, Sir, to give it up, if it is for Your Majesty's service. And as a mark of it, if Mr. Pitt had thought proper to have taken any other employment for himself ; and Your Majesty had been pleased to continue me in the office, where I am, I should have humbly beg'd Your Majesty's leave to retire. My age makes me wish it, and the only inducement I had to return to Your Majesty's service, was the hopes of being able to be of some service to Your Majesty, and use to your present Ministers ; that that was not now the case ; that I sincerely thought Mr. Pitt had no occasion for my advice ; and that, if he had, I was sure he would not take it ; and therefore my remaining in employment could be of no use to Your Majesty, or the publick ; and the loss of it could not give me the least uneasiness, as I have the satisfaction of having so lately received that gracious declaration from Your Majesty, ' That I had done more service to your Royal Family than anyone had done from the year 1714 ;' and that Your Majesty has been graciously pleased to tell me ' How satisfied you was with my conduct, since you was last pleased to re-admit me into your service.'

These declarations, so much for my own honor and justification, I hoped His Majesty would have no objection to then being known. To which the King very readily agreed. As to the manner, Sir, I cannot say it is the most agreable to me. *Where is that bed of roses which Mr. Pitt promised me?*[1] And there I left it.'

The King then went on, Mr. Pitt *will have* my Lord Camden Chancellor; I told him I could not turn out my Lord Northington. Mr. Pitt said I don't desire you, Sir; except my Ld. Northington will consent to be President, and, said the King, my Lord Northington has told me that he is always ready to make me easy; and he has accepted the President of the Council.

I own this Law disposition surprized me extremely, upon many accounts, remembering what I had heard often from His Majesty upon that subject; and having never heard one word of it, or of any such design either from Mr. Conway or from anybody else 'till that moment.

It did occur to me, tho' I did not mention it to the King, that His Majesty might as well have said to Mr. Pitt when he desired my place, that he could not turn out an old servant, under the description, that he had often made of me *himself, without my consent*; and that the offer of the place, since it was to be vacated, might, to save appearances, have been made to me; which might have been done very safely; for no consideration upon earth should have made me accept it.

The King then told me that the Earl of Shelburne was to be Secretary of State in the room of the Duke of Richmond; and, His Majesty added, And *he will make a very good one*. To which I replied, *My Lord Shelburne, Sir, has very good parts.*

I should have observed at first, that His Majesty told me, that this new administration was to be founded upon the present administration; as Mr. Pitt had said to Mr. Conway in his first conversation.

I then, as it was my duty, in consequence of the charge which His Majesty had honor'd me with, expressed my hopes, that upon the death of the Bishop of Salisbury,[2] His Majesty would be pleased to carry into execution the scheme which His

. *Chatham Correspondence*, ii. 408.   [2] John Thomas, died July 20, 1766

Majesty had approved ; (and, as far as relates to the Bishop of Oxford,[1] was mentioned to me first by the King). The scheme was viz. the Bishop of Oxford to Salisbury, the Bishop of St. David's[2] to Oxford, and Dr. Moss to St. David's. I had got Dr. Lowth's promise *previously* to remove to Oxford, tho' the value was equal or rather less. His Majesty was extremely pleased with that, as well as with the proposal, that Dr. Moss should be Bishop of St. David's.[3] This shows how much the King did then approve the scheme. His Majesty seemed to make some difficulty now ; and said he would consider of it.

I could not avoid representing to the King how much I should be mortified, if His Majesty, before I was dismissed from my office, and when I was in possession of his gracious commands to recommend proper persons on all these vacancies, should alter his very kind intentions to the Bishop of Oxford. And I added one argument which I hoped might have weight with His Majesty, that the Dutchess of Newcastle, who has been the best friend, and best wife to me for forty-five, and I might have said, forty-nine years,[4] had this so much at heart, that I did not know how the disappointment might affect her health. But all I could say produced no other answer, than that *His Majesty would consider of it*, with regard to me.

I cannot but look upon this as the most cruel treatment that ever man met with ; especially after my services to His Majesty's Royal Family for over fifty years, so lately and so strongly acknowledged *by the King himself to me*.

Whether this be the Act of the new Minister or not is little material, for I will suppose that His Majesty can have no other reason for mortifying me in this manner, and departing from what he intended, but the fear of disobliging Mr. Pitt.

---

[1] John Hume, who succeeded to Salisbury, 1766.
[2] Robert Lowth, who succeeded to Oxford, 1766.
[3] Dr. Charles Moss became Bishop of St. David's, 1766.
[4] They were married April 2, 1717.

This, if it should be the case, shows the extensive power and influence of Mr. Pitt; which I hope for the sake of the publick he will use with more humanity, and with greater regard to merit and long services upon other occasions than he has done upon this.

The King told me that the alterations would be declared next week. When I deliver the Privy Seal I shall say what I think my own honor, and my duty to the King, and my country, require of me.

In these circumstances, I considered what was to be done; and as I knew the Archbp. of Canterbury would do everything in the world, that was friendly to me; and as His Grace was, by the King, joined in commission with me, I desired he would wait upon His Majesty, on Friday last, (which he did) and the enclosed [1] copy of the Archbishop's [2] letter, sent to me immediately upon his coming from court, will inform you, that His Majesty had been pleased, with great chearfulness, and strong expressions of regard to me, to do what I had proposed, with relation to the Bishops.

I imagined, however, that Mr. Pitt had been consulted; and I since know (and the owning it makes it rather better than worse) that the King told the Archbishop that His Majesty, being on the point of taking Mr. Pitt *for his Minister*, did not think it would be proper for him to take such a step as this without previously acquainting his intended Minister with it; and that he had done so, and was now ready to agree to what had been proposed. And this was the reason for his not doing it *immediately*.

I believe I can acquaint you with an anecdote that may give some farther light upon this transaction.

The Bishop of Oxford, much affected with what had passed, and knowing that his friend, my Lord Lincoln, was Mr. Pitt's first

---

[1] A reference to the Appendix. [2] Secker.

favorite, asked my leave to desire the assistance of my Lord Lincoln in it, with Mr. Pitt.

As I really wished the poor Bishop success, I readily gave it, peremptorily insisting that my name should not, on any account, be made use of, either to my Lord Lincoln, or Mr. Pitt.

Thus this affair ended, and tho' attended with many disagreable circumstances to me, both as to substance and manner, I shall make my proper acknowledgements to the King, for His Majesty's having been graciously pleased to comply with my request; and I shall endeavour to conceal, as far as I can, that part of this transaction which could not be agreable to me.

I am told that the new administration is to be declared on Wensday; tho' I have not yet received any orders from His Majesty to bring the Privy Seal.

I hear this morning, that Chas. Townshend had accepted the Chancellor of the Exchequer; as he says the reason for his changing his mind was the King's asking it of him; and that Mr. Dowdeswell was to be well taken care of.[1] I am very glad of it, for Mr. Dowdeswell's sake, but that is nothing to the publick.

I have now given you a full account of all I know of the intended dismission of the present administration, and the appointments of the new one.

What consequences this may have with regard to others who remain in employment, whether any of them are to be removed, or may intend to resign their employments, I do not know. My own opinion is against resignations for the sake of the party, the cause, and in some cases, for the sake of my poor friends themselves.

You will see by the enclosed letters all that I know upon that subject. I send you a copy of a letter from Mr. West [2] with an

---

[1] See below, p. 96.   [2] A reference to the Appendix.

account of an extraordinary conversation with my Lord Camden. All that I can say of it is, that as far as it relates to myself, it is *Declaratio contra factum.*

Fo. 86 b.   Claremont : August 4, 1766.

I shall now proceed to acquaint you with what passed in the closet upon my delivering the Privy Seal on Wensday, the 30th of July, to His Majesty, in consequence of a very civil letter which I had received from Mr. Conway, of which I send you a copy; and also of my answer.[1]

As soon as I came into the closet, I acquainted His Majesty that I was come, in obedience to his commands, to deliver the Privy Seal to him, and to thank His Majesty for his reception of my services, and the marks of confidence which I had received from him, during the time that I had held it. The King replied in the most gracious manner, that he had all the regard for me possible and that *that* was not at all altered by what had happen'd, and *that* he should preserve, without the least diminution, at all times; that what had happened did not proceed from the least disregard to me, or alteration of his opinion upon my subject.

I told His Majesty that *that* being the case, I was extremely easy and happy. That when I took the Privy Seal, it was from an opinion, that, from my long experience, I might be of some service to his Ministers, who might not have had so much experience as myself; men whom I honor'd and loved; and some of whom had been bred up by me. That that was not now the case, and that therefore as I could be of no service to His Majesty's affairs, I retired with great pleasure and satisfaction; that I should always have the same duty and regard for His Majesty in my private station, as I had when I had the honor to be in his service, and most sincerely wished His Majesty a

---

[1] References to the Appendix.

long, happy, and glorious reign ; and that every thing might be done to His Majesty's honor and interest.

The King interrupted me; he seemed extremely pleased with what I had said, and have *attempted*, and [1] in the beginning, would have said, as he did afterwards, that he was extremely glad to do what he had done for the Bishop of Oxford, as it pleased me ; but he owned he had another inducement to it, and that was, that he knew it would be agreable *to the Dutchess of Newcastle ; and desired me to tell her so from him.* Upon which I repeated my thanks to His Majesty.

I told the King I had *had a hint* for which I was much obliged to His Majesty, and that I hoped that whatever answer I might have given to it, His Majesty would not think it proceeded from any want of duty or regard to him.

I recommended the University of Cambridge,[2] and the deserving men there, to His Majesty's royal favor ; of which His Majesty was pleased to assure me.

I observed how much the University would fear, that they should be sufferers by my being out of His Majesty's service ; that in order to give me some consolation for them, at my going out, I hoped His Majesty would allow me to recommend to him my very deserving friend, Dr. Powell, our present Vice-Chancellor,[3] (whom I had often before mentioned to His Majesty, as a man of great merit,, for the Archdeaconry of Colchester, value about two hundred pounds pr. ann.: which would be vacated by the promotion of Dr. Moss.

His Majesty, with the greatest readiness and pleasure, said he would do it, and told Mr. Secretary Conway of it upon his coming into the closet immediately after.

I observed to the King, that it was but a trifle, with regard to the just pretension Dr. Powell had to His Majesty's favor : but small as it was, as I was just leaving his service, it would

---

[1] MS. *attempted it.*   [2] The Duke was Chancellor.
[3] Master of St. John's College, Cambridge. He obtained the Archdeaconry.

be a great pleasure to me, to have had an opportunity of shewing my regard to so deserving a man as Dr. Powell.

I took the liberty to recommend my friends to His Majesty; if, by their conduct, they should deserve His Majesty's favor. I particularly mentioned my cousin Pelham, and hoped, in a proper time, His Majesty would consider him.

His Majesty was not at all displeased with what I had said; and seemed to shew a very good disposition towards my friends.

I then told the King, that, as this would probably be the last time, that I should come into His Majesty's closet, as one of his servants, (the King replied very graciously, ' I hope you mean it in that sense only ') I would take the liberty to advise him, to keep as many of *his old servants as he could.* His Majesty seemed, by his manner, to agree to it.

I told him I knew them all; that they were, and that His Majesty would find them so, at the end, His Majesty's best and truest friends.

I had kissed the King's hand at first, upon delivering the Privy Seal to him.

Having now finished the account of my proceedings at court, upon my resignation of the Privy Seal, I shall inform you, as shortly as I can, of the dispositions that have been made in consequence of the removals, or filling up of employments, that have been some time vacant.[1]

Mr. James Grenville has accepted one of the Vice-Treasurers of Ireland; Col. Barré and Mr. Oswald have the other two, so that my Lord George Sackville is removed.

The Pay Office is to be divided; Lord North has accepted half paymaster, and the other half was offered to Mr. Dowdeswell, who has refused it; and it has since been given to Mr. George Cooke, of Middlesex.

Lord Dartmouth has resigned the First Lord Commissioner

---

[1] On these appointments see *Walpole* (Barker), ii. 253 *sqq.*, and *Letters*, v. 8.

of Trade; as Mr. Pitt had opposed making a third Secretary of State for the plantations, which had been promised to my Lord Dartmouth. The First Commissioner of Trade has been offer'd to Mr. Dowdeswell, and has been refused; and is since given to my Lord Hillsborough.

It is thought that Sir Charles Saunders and Sir William Meredith will resign their places at the Admiralty, which I am very sorry for. Mr. John Yorke has already resigned his seat at the Admiralty Board, as Sir Chas. Saunders and my Lord Egmont have since done.

I cannot too much commend the generosity, (I will call it,) a noble way of thinking, of our friend, the Duke of Portland, in resisting his own inclinations, by keeping his employment for the sake of the publick, and the Whig cause.

Had His Grace consulted his own inclination only, I am persuaded so many resignations would have followed, as would undoubtedly have thrown the Earl of Chatham into those hands, from whom every violence and destruction to the Whig cause, was to be expected.

The Duke of Richmond, Mr. Dowdeswell, and some few of us, dined with my Lord Rockingham, on Saturday, and yesterday the Marquess of Rockingham, Lord Albemarle, Admiral Keppel, Lord Bessborough, Lord Grantham, Lord Gage, Sir Anthony Abdy, Sir William Meredith, Mr. Burton of the Bank, and Mr. Burke, dined here.

Union amongst all our friends was unanimously agreed upon; and I preached strongly against opposition; at least against any formed or formal opposition; and I think that was the general sense of the company. And I am of opinion that the interest of the publick, and our own honor, engage us not to oppose the men, and the measures, of those we have acted with, as long as they shall act upon *the same principles*, and pursue the same measures.

It is said, that, at present, at least, the Earl of Chatham to a degree has lost his popularity both in the City, and in the country, by his coming up to the House of Lords.

Sir Anthony Abdy told me that he met Humphrey Coates[1] and Glover[2] yesterday morning, who told him, that they had got the pamphlet[3] which has been advertized against Mr. Pitt, with a full account of what had passed, (I suppose,) with Lord Temple; and that they were carrying it to Almon to be printed. Sir Anthony asked them whether it was *authentick*? And they said *yes*. What will become of all this I can't pretend to foresee.

Mr. Chas. Yorke has resigned the office of Attorney General. He had a long audience of the King, and I find, by my Lord Rockingham, that he acted with great spirit and propriety. It is thought he will quit his business in Westminster Hall. His brother John has resigned,[4] and I have received a very kind, and a very strong letter, from my Lord Hardwicke.

Everybody seemed pleased with the promotion of Judge Wilmot, to be Chief Justice of the Common Pleas. I own it surprized me, and I did not, nor do yet know, from whence it comes; it is given to our new young Minister my Lord Shelburne. Our friends are particularly pleased with Mr. Willes;[5] they say he is a very good Whig; and has given great proofs of his being a good friend.

I have now stated to you, and for the Duke of Portland's perusal, all the facts that have come to my knowledge. You now see a full deduction of the whole; and I hope you will not be so cautious as not to send me your opinion in general, in

---

[1] The notorious Humphrey Cotes. See Walpole's *Letters*, iv. 125.
[2] Richard Glover, M.P., another friend of Lord Temple's.
[3] 'An Inquiry into the Conduct of a late Right Honourable Commoner,' on which see *Grenville Correspondence*, iii. 292, and *Walpole* (Barker), ii. 245. Humphrey Cotes and Almon are believed to have written it from materials supplied by Lord Temple.
[4] As Lord Commissioner of the Admiralty.
[5] Who was made Solicitor-General.

return for the very great pains which I have been at, to put things together in one light ; that the Duke of Portland, and yourself may let me have your opinion upon the whole, and especially as to my own conduct ; for I have now nothing in view, nor to wish, but to be able, in my private station to serve the *publick*, and the Whig cause ; and to preserve the good opinion and approbation of my friends, and particularly of my two best friends, the Duke of Portland, and yourself.

I hear the *offer* or *no offer*[1] of the pension,[2] and *my certain refusal*, is much approved, and particularly by the Duke of Bedford, who told my Lord Albemarle, it was the greatest and noblest part that ever man acted, and *what he should have expected from me*, or to that effect.

I will fling out only one hint ; should, as is very possible, the Earl of Chatham, upon appearances not answering expectation, return to Pynsent,[3] what would then become of the publick ? And whose hands would it be flung into ?

As I don't know what particular expressions there may be in the letters enclosed, I should wish they might be seen by nobody but yourself, and the Duke of Portland. I must leave it to you to communicate this narrative, or such parts only as you may think proper, to my Whig friends, Sir George Savile and Mr. Hewett.

The Dutchess of Newcastle desires her kindest compliments to you, and the Duke of Portland, and we both beg you would, in a most particular manner, assure the whole house of Chatsworth, lords, ladies, and gentlemen, of the attachment of Claremont to them, and to every thing that comes there including *Wolterton*.[4]

I intend to trouble my good friend Lord George,[5] with a

---

[1] See below, p. 150.
[2] On the Duke's refusal of the pension of 4000*l*. see *Grenville Correspondence*, iii. 291, and *Walpole* (Barker), ii. 253.
[3] In Somerset.
[4] Wolterton was Lord Orford's place. The allusion is to seek.
[5] Lord George Cavendish.

letter to thank him for his kind remembrances of me, in his letter to Lord John.[1]

Lord George knows the sincere friendship and regard I have for him ; which he is, every day, giving me reason to increase.

XIII

Fo. 288. Claremont : July 6, 1767.

MR. WHITE,—DEAR SIR,—The session of Parliament being now ended ; and some plan for patching up the present administration, by removals amongst themselves, or forming a new one,[2] being now under consideration, I shall, according to my promise, send you a narrative of the most material occurrences which have come to my knowledge, both with respect to the proceedings in parliament, since you left us in May, or any other points relating to the present situation of publick affairs and the disposition of the several parties towards them.

On the 13th of May I had a very material conversation with my Lord Mansfield.

I shewed His Lordship Mr. West's first account of what had passed that day in the House of Commons upon the American affairs, and Mr. Charles Townshend's motions.

My Lord Mansfield was very clear in disapproving the motion for restraining the Governor of New York from giving his assent to any Act of Assembly ;[3] and was much inclined to approve, what was flung out by Mr. Dowdeswell, for enforcing the quartering of troops. He said, he had had some discourse with G. Grenville ; that he could not very well tell, what his

---

[1] Lord John Cavendish.

[2] There are several accounts of Wharton's negotiation with Rockingham, and through his party with the Bedford and Grenville party, herein explained in detail by the Duke of Newcastle. Cf. *Grenville Correspondence*, especially the letter of July 6, 1767, to Lord Temple, iv. 31 ; *Bedford Correspondence*, iii. 365-390 ; Cavendish's *Debates*, p. 582 *sqq.* ; Phillimore's *Lyttelton*, ii. 723 *sqq.* ; Almon's *Anecdotes of the Earl of Chatham*, ii. 51 *sqq.* : Walpole's *Letters*, v. 55.

[3] Cf. *Walpole* (Barker), iii. 28, note 2.

notion was, but he thought, he was of opinion, that the complying colonies, and meritorious persons in them, should receive some marks of favor from the Government.

That Mr. Grenville would not give in to Mr. Townshend's proposal, on any account: but he thought, he would come into Mr. Dowdeswell's proposition; that Mr. Grenville had some notion of adding to the oath of allegiance, and their swearing to abide by the declaratory law, relating to the superiority of this country over the colonies: but Lord Mansfield did not seem to approve it.

My Lord Mansfield thought, that, both as to the affairs of the East India Company and the general state of America, nothing could properly be done in the House of Lords, 'till we saw, what the House of Commons would do in it; but that, as to the Act of Indemnity, and compensation, we should have the resolutions of the King in Council laid before us; which Lord Gower would move for tomorrow; that by the account he had had of the resolution of the Council, he did, by no means, approve of it. That my Lord Chief Justice Wilmot was absolutely for declaring the Act of Assembly *null* and *void*, as to the indemnity, and good, as to the compensation. That, when the resolution of the Council came to be considered in the House of Lords, he was of opinion, that the House should declare three things,

First, That that part of the Act, which relates to the indemnity, was null, and void; which would be the best proof of the opinion of the House, that the Assemblies of the Colonies have not equal power with the Parliament of Great Britain.

Secondly, That that part of the Act was in itself null, and void; but the other part, with regard to the compensation, which had no relation to it, stood good, valid, and unimpeached

Thirdly, That the King in Council has a right in Acts of Assemblies to reject any one independent part, and take the other; for that in those Acts of Assemblies, independent parts of them, are, and must be, looked upon as distinct Acts; or otherwise, the Assemblies would have it in their power, to cramb whatever acts they please down here, or the necessary acts of government could not be passed; which is contrary to the very constitution of the colonies.

That there should be these resolutions of the House of Lords, when the resolutions of the Council should come to be considered.

By this you will see, what points were then under consideration, and the opinions of the several persons therein named upon them.

When these points came into the House of Lords, we had several divisions upon them; in some of which we brought our numbers in the committee (not including proxies) to a majority of only three on the side of the court.[1]

This gave us very great courage, and determined us to exert all our strength; and the Duke of Bedford and all his friends, my Lord Mansfield, and all our friends, acted most cordially together upon every question. This union, and activity on our part, getting so near them, as by the difference of three votes only, the court exerted all their power, and mustered up all their friends. The Duke of Grafton as first Minister, and at the head of the whole, was indefatigable, and, to do him justice, shewed great resolution; the power of the court was so strong, that our late division upon, I think, the most unjust and most destructive bill, with regard to private property and publick credit, I mean the Dividend Bill,[2] was carried by much greater majorities, than the other questions had been.

Some of those, who had voted with us, left us; and many, or at least some, were brought up who had either not appeared in parliament for some years, and some who had scarce ever voted before.

---

[1] Cf. *Walpole* (Barker), iii. 35, in the division on the Massachusetts Act.

[2] Dyson's bill for regulating the East India directors' dividends. Cf. *Walpole* (Barker), iii. 16, 36, 41, 42.

And thus, notwithstanding the clearest, the strongest arguments which were most ably made use of, and enforced upon every point by my Lord Mansfield particularly, by my Lord Weymouth (who is one of the most promising young men,[1] that I ever knew in the House of Lords,) and the Duke of Richmond (who with time and a little more experience, and deference to the opinion of others, who have it, will also be very considerable), the bill was carried.

Upon the first question, that a conference be desired with the Commons upon the Dividend Bill, the numbers for it were 57, to 98 against it.

Upon the second question to amend the bill by leaving out the words 24th of June 1767, and instead thereof inserting the 25th of December next, the numbers were 44 for it and 59 against it.

And thus the session ended. His Majesty's speech will shew you the judgment that is made upon it. I cannot say that I can find out the many great things that have been done, this session, for the good of the publick.

You will have heard that Chas. Townshend, and Mr. Conway acted in direct opposition to the Ministry, at the head of which was Mr. Dyson, and to the last opposed the Dividend Bill, of which the Duke of Grafton declared himself the friend and patron.

During this fluctuation which was in both Houses, various reports were every day spread, with regard to the forming a new administration, or patching up the old one. The Duke of Grafton was declared to be the principal person that was to prepare or form that plan.

Lord Chatham was supposed to be pretty much out of the question; and was either to be left in his place or retire by his own consent, as they should think most for the service.

---

[1] Walpole's 'inconsiderable, debauched young man (Barker, ii. 126).

Lord Bute was gone out of town, but Mr. Mackenzie was every day in the House of Lords, and every day in close conference with the Duke of Grafton ; all Lord Bute's friends, Lord Talbot, Sir G. Elliot, Dyson were mightily extolling the Duke of Grafton ; and His Grace was received and talked of at court in the highest light ; my nephew, Onslow, and all the Duke of Grafton's friends, saying publickly, that the Duke of Grafton's plan was to take in his old friends, Lord Rockingham etc. ; and that it should not be his fault, if it did not succeed.

These reports were followed by overtures, (if they can be called such,) made by General Conway, (as appeared afterwards, though my Lord Rockingham would never have confidence enough in me, to name the person) to my Lord Rockingham ; and, in some measure, to many of our friends, who dined with Mr. Conway at my Lord Rockingham's last Friday.

You will see an account of what passed by the following letters, inserted in the body of this letter, to make the narrative more compleat.

Fo. 293.   ' Peterboro' House : July 4, 1767.

'MY DEAR LORD,—I could not write to your Grace yesterday in the morning, I had nothing to communicate ; and I shall now give you an account of what passed in the evening. Your Grace knows, for some days past, it has been the conversation that the Duke of Grafton wished to see his old friends back in administration, and that it was his inclination to bring it about, and, at the same time, wishing that those, who held the conversation, would try to sound our thoughts.

'This has grown more and more, insomuch that yesterday evening, I was told that the Duke of Grafton would be ready to converse on the subject of forming an administration, if we could only inform him whether we had any intention, or desire, of moving the Commander in Chief, Lord Granby, or the Chancellor, Lord Camden ; that in either of those cases, it was difficult to come to any agreement.¹ This had been casually thrown out before, but I had avoided giving any information, not from thinking the *Army* would occasion much difficulty, as I have long known Lord Albemarle's sentiments on that matter. And in regard to the *Law*, I did not think it would be at all necessary to give answers to vague and undefined propositions.

'I think as far and as well as I can recollect, the Duke of Grafton's idea is to take any, or even no office, just as may be wished, which, to be sure, personally from himself, is exceeding handsome.

'Yesterday evening's conversation was more explicit, and yet not fully so, upon the subject of Lord Chatham. He is considered as quite out of the question, and I think the conversation goes to his retiring out of place; but even that is hardly positive; but enough for us to conclude it was so intended, either of his own motion, or some how or other.

'Nothing that has dropped seems to go farther than a treaty with *us*. And nothing drops in regard to His Majesty, but only as the Duke of Grafton's opinion, that His Majesty's preference is to us.

'Your Grace saw, in the House of Lords, that Lord Northington took out Lord Gower. I don't understand that any thing specifick passed, but probably a similar conversation to what has been thrown out to us.

'Indeed it was said to me, that if we were shy, and would not shew a readiness to treat, the probability was, that treaty might be carried on elsewhere.

'The Duke of Portland, Lord Winchilsea, General Conway, Lord Albemarle, and the Cavendishes, and Mr. Dowdeswell dined with me yesterday. We talked this matter over amongst us, and before General Conway, who much wishes to see a plan

¹ Cf. *Grenville Correspondence*, iv. 37. It was thought that the Rockingham party made it a condition that Yorke should be Chancellor and Lord Albemarle head of the army.

formed: but, I think, the opinion was, that, without more information, if any specifick answer was to be given it could not prudently be done. That it was wished, by us, to know whether a general and solid plan was the object; and in that case (tho' under no engagements) we should desire to talk with the Bedfords etc. That if it was only meant to make a few changes, and not a solid plan, we would much prefer seeing any set, or sets, undertake administration, on such a foot, than be the undertakers ourselves.

'It was thrown out that Mr. Yorke might, (upon our assenting to the Chancellor remaining etc.) be a Peer and President.

'Indeed, upon the whole, it strikes me, that the present administration is at a loss how to turn themselves; and that the closet is much in that situation, and that now they are sounding about by way of separate treaties. And I own my opinion is that we ought to be cautious, and 'till more light is given say as little as may be.

'I supped at Lord Albemarle's with Lord Gower and Lord Weymouth, and gave them communication. Lord Gower told me he had refer'd Lord Northington to the Duke of Bedford, and that he knows nothing farther about it. What may ensue is scarce to be foreseen. I think, if the negotiation is thrown into our hands, we may possibly succeed in persuading the Duke of Bedford's friends to take part with us. If, on the contrary, the negotiation is thrown into the Duke of Bedford's etc., they must, of course, make their point, G. Grenville; and in that case, G. Grenville and Lord Temple will take the lead in administration; or else the Duke of Grafton will be so pressed etc. that he, and this administration, will try to go on, with some few alterations of office among themselves.

'If I was to guess, of the three ways, which was least likely to happen, I should think a negotiation with the Duke of Bedford etc., allowing them to put George Grenville at the head, is the most unlikely. I shall certainly wait upon your Grace to-morrow, and bring you what farther intelligence I hear, tho' probably, as I stay here tonight, I shall know nothing farther.

'I am etc.

ROCKINGHAM.

' P.S.—There are parts of this letter which, when I see your Grace, I will mention to you, as more secret than other parts.'[1]

To this letter I sent the following answer.

Fo. 296 b. July 4, 1767.

MY DEAR LORD,—I am very much obliged to your Lordship for your kind communication. I have expected it for some days. I was almost certain, that something of this sort was upon the anvil; and, by what the Duke of Richmond said to me, of Genl Conway's way of thinking, I imagined, it would end in some overture of this sort, from the Duke of Grafton.

When I have the honor of seeing your Lordship tomorrow, (and I hope you will come early for that purpose,) I shall know some particulars, which may enable me to form a better judgment, than I can possibly do at present.

The two points insisted upon, of Lord Granby and the Chancellor, are, I believe, the Duke of Grafton's own. As to the first, if my Lord Albemarle is satisfied with it, I can have no objection to it. As to the other, your Lordship knows more of the Yorkes than I do:—but so much, I think, I know, that they will never be satisfied, 'till Charles Yorke has the Great Seal. But there is another difficulty, which, I am sure, will have great weight with your Lordship, as it has, and must have, with me. My Lord Mansfield will, with reason, be highly offended at it; and will think, that it is meant, as, I believe, it is, (considering the quarter from whence it comes,) as a personal affront to him; and, I am sure, the loss of my Lord Mansfield to the publick and our friends, will be of greater consequence, than ten thousand Granbys, and Camdens.

[1] Perhaps some of the ' etceteras ' of the above.

When I have a full conversation with your Lordship tomorrow, and know your own thoughts upon it, I will give you mine, with all sincerity, coolness, attention and good wishes, to you and your friends, that I am capable of. I suppose you don't think of going soon to Yorkshire. This will require attendence [*sic*] and concert.

I am, my dear Lord, etc.

The next morning, I received the following letter from my Lord Albemarle.

Fo. 298. 'Arlington Street : July 4, 1767, Saturday evening.

'MY LORD,—I am ashamed to have let your fishman go to-day, without expressing my concern for the Dutchess of Newcastle's health. I hope it is no more than the common cold, and of the mildest sort; and that Her Grace has received so much benefit from her bleeding, as not to want a repetition of it.

'I must now give you the reason for my neglect, and hope you will excuse me. The Marquess,[1] that eternal setter up debauched me 'till four in the morning, upon a message or a something from the Duke of Grafton, thro' Conway, which he communicated to his company yesterday. It was thought right by the Duke of Portland, Earl of Winchilsea, Dowdeswell and myself, the four last remaining, to inform the Bedfords of it immediately, and keep up that confidence and good understanding that subsists between us. I was commissioned to find out Gower and Rigby; and give them a bottle of wine at my house, where the Marquess was to inform them of all he knew. Rigby is at Wooburne ; I desired Gower to bring Weymouth. The Marquess was very frank and open. I don't think they received the information so cordially as I wished. For God sake, my Lord, keep this to yourself, I may be mistaken : I hope I am.

[1] Of Rockingham.

'The conversation was general, I mean on politicks; no professions from either side; we parted very good friends at four this morning, and I am yet alive. The Marquess, whom I know nothing of today, will give *you all the* particulars, too long, as they were not very interesting, to write.

'I go to Buxton tomorrow, very truly and faithfully the Duke of Newcastle's humble servant. May I beg my respects to the Dutchess and that your Grace will believe me, most sincerely, etc.

'ALBEMARLE.'

In this situation the Marquess came hither yesterday; and there met him, or came with him, my Lord Winchilsea, the Duke of Portland, Lord Bessborough, Lord Frederick and Lord John Cavendish. Poor Lord George had an accident, as you know, in his eye, which prevented him. He is, I thank God, pure well; and sets out, for Lancashire, on Tuesday next. Lord Rockingham and my Lord Winchilsea came together. I had a good deal of discourse with them two alone. Little new passed; I urged the necessity of taking the Bedfords with us; in which I was strongly supported by good Lord Winchilsea. Lord Rockingham did not object to it; and has shewed, by his subsequent behaviour, that he acts entirely upon that principle; and I do not despair of success.

Little material passed, and nothing new from the quarter of the court. A good inclination was in all the company to take in the Bedfords, tho' strong declarations from some of them against G. Grenville.

The two next letters from my Lord Rockingham bring things to a point, [at] which, I own, I scarce ever expected to see them — an offer, from the King, of the Treasury to my Lord Rockingham; and an admission, on the part of the Duke of Grafton, that Lord Rockingham, according to his proposal, should be at liberty to communicate what had passed to the Duke of Bedford.

The letters themselves, here inserted, will shew you fully all that has passed.

'Grosvenor Square: July 7, 1767.

'MY DEAR LORD,—I had a message conveyed to me yesterday, that the Duke of Grafton would meet me today at 2 o'clock at Gen¹. Conway's, and, as I understand, authorized by His Majesty. I shall try to be more a hearer than speaker upon the occasion, in order to know, as much as I can, what their ideas now are. I do not expect much to pass, but whether much or little I shall send your Grace an account tonight. I am etc.

'ROCKINGHAM.'

Fo. 300.   'Grosvenor Square: July 7, 1767 (late that night).

'MY DEAR LORD,—I just send your Grace a short account of the result of this day. I met the Duke of Grafton at Mr. Conway's; and began by complimenting His Grace upon the handsome part he acted in this matter, and took occasion to say, that, last year, our only difference arose in regard to Ld. Chatham etc. That I attributed what had happened since, to have ensued from the same cause etc.

'His Grace then opened what he was authorized to say from His Majesty; and which amounted to a proposition, that we should come into administration, along with the *remains* of the present administration. That our friends should come into office and that His Majesty desired a plan might be formed to be laid before him.

'I desired to know whether we might try the Duke of Bedford's friends, and found that it was understood we would—and no objection to it. In regard to G. Grenville etc. an implied exclusion.

'*Remains of the present* administration, I found *particularly* was relative to Ld. Camden—tho' much caution in regard to others, by way of preventing at this moment it being said, that His Majesty gave up A, B or C etc.

'The Treasury offered to me, the Duke of Grafton inclined either to take office or not, according as it might appear to us advantageous for the administration.

'I shall send an express to Lord Albemarle, who leaves Wooburn tomorrow morning, and shall desire him to have a full conversation with the Duke of Bedford, and shall wish Lord Albemarle to stay a day or two for his assistance there. I can consider this only more as an opening, than, as yet, any thing on which a judgment can be formed. The material matter is, how far His Majesty will incline to allow us to introduce a number sufficient to give real strength. If that can't be, I own, I shall have no desire to be a part. I am etc.

'ROCKINGHAM.'

Upon these letters you will see my sentiments, by the following answer.

Fo. 301 b.   Claremont: July 8, 1767.

MY DEAR LORD,—Just as I was got into bed, last night, your Lordship's servant brought me your letter; I was impatient to read it as your Lordship may imagine; and I have the pleasure to tell you, that it gave me more satisfaction than I expected to receive from the first overture.

The King sending his Minister to your Lordship to open the negotiation, and with an offer of the first employment in England to your Lordship: and His Majesty desiring that a plan might be formed to be laid before him, was, to be sure, a good setting out: but that which gave me the most satisfaction, was the very prudent and honorable part, which your Lordship took on that occasion; and from whence I conceive great good, whatever may be the event of this negotiation.

Your Lordship opened your conference very dextrously by

touching the vanity of the young Minister in a manner which plainly had it's effect ; but that which gave me the most solid comfort, was your Lordship's proposal, to try the Duke of Bedford's friends ; and to find that *it was understood that you would, and that no objection would be made to it.*

This shews your Lordship's own inclination ; and also gives reason to hope that, if that method is pursued with firmness, it may succeed ; and nothing could be more proper than your immediately employing my Lord Albemarle, (who, I hope, is now at Woburn) for that purpose. I am persuaded that your Lordship's instructions to Lord Albemarle will be proper and full, and I will answer for his zeal in the execution of them. If that plan succeeds, the business is over, and we shall soon see such an administration formed, as may answer the expectations of all those, who really wish the honor and interest of their country, and the peace and quiet of the kingdom. As an inducement to it, I will venture to give it as my opinion, that neither the Duke of Bedford and his friends, nor (if you will give me leave to say so) your Lordship, and your friends, can, without each other, form such an administration, as can last, and do the business of the publick, without absolutely depending upon my Lord Bute for its success and duration, and *that* I am persuaded, neither the Duke of Bedford, nor your Lordship will consent to.

I am sorry to find that the Duke of Grafton said nothing upon the subject of my Lord Bute. *That* must in the course of the negotiation be fully explained. I suppose, what was said about Lord Chatham, will be confirmed, so that His Lordship will be really out of the question.

As a most sincere friend and well-wisher to your Lordship I must hope and indeed I do not doubt, but that you will carry my Lord Mansfield with you, in whatever you do. You have already very wisely communicated to him the disagreable part relating to my Lord Camden. For my own part, I neither see the necessity, nor the use of keeping him. He has lost all his credit, by his speeches about the dispensing power;[1] and the little regard he shewed to private property, or publick credit, in his late debates in support of the Dividend Bill. But, if my Lord Mansfield and your other friends should consent to it, there is a much easier way of doing it by letting him succeed his friend, my Lord Northington, as President of the Council; and giving the Seals, as you always intended, to Mr. Charles Yorke; and surely this ought to satisfy my Lord Camden.

What I say of my Lord Mansfield is from opinion, and knowledge of his superior talents. Your Lordship, I know, has his heart; and his head will be found absolutely necessary, in the present circumstances for the support of any administration that means to act with dignity and success for the honor and interest of the nation, the ease, quiet, and credit of the King; and, I believe, what relates to my Lord Mansfield, will not be disagreable to His Majesty.[2]

As I mean, by this letter, to fling out my thoughts to your Lordship in these early days of this negotiation, upon every point, that may deserve your Lordship's attention and consideration, I shall necessarily make it very long, and for that reason, I have chosen to write it myself, and have it copied for your Lordship in honest and faithful Dr. Hurdis's[3] hand, that your Lordship may read it without any difficulty;[4] and give it that weight and consideration which your Lordship may think it may deserve.

As an old Minister, and one who has been bred up in

---

[1] Cf. *Parl. Hist.* xvi. 350; Almon's *Anecdotes of Eminent Persons*, i. 376; *Lyttelton*, ii. 710.

[2] Cf. Walpole on Lord Mansfield's 'superior cowardice and superior abilities (*George III*, ii. 280).

[3] Thomas Hurdis, D.D., the Duke's chaplain.

[4] The Duke's handwriting became almost illegible.

thinking, that this country could not subsist without proper alliances, and connections with foreign powers, I have seen with the utmost concern the total neglect of foreign affairs, even by my Lord Chatham, who raised himself and his reputation by a contrary conduct. If ever this consideration became necessary, I am sorry to say, I *know*, it is so now. I don't pretend to say what, or with whom, those alliances or those connections should be made; that must depend upon circumstances, and the condition and disposition of the respective powers; but I mean all such connections to be formed upon the principle of preserving the peace, as Sir Robert Walpole, that enemy to foreign connections, always said, *Preventive and Defensive*.

I have had such an account of the present state of France, as must almost make every good Englishman tremble; or at least think it is high time to look about us. France, everybody knows, is absolutely master of Spain; and those two monarchies as effectually united as if they were under one head.

The Duc de Choiseul, the present sole Minister, *absolute, bold, able*, and *enterprizing*; and I suppose, no friend in his heart to us. Their army compleat to a man, well officered, well appointed and well paid; their trade flourishing everywhere and encroaching on our's. And I am afraid, after what has lately passed, their publick credit as stable as our's, so that they are in a condition *to strike* whenever the moment comes, that they shall think proper to do it.

These evils are easier seen than the remedy to be suggested; I only fling them out as what demand the immediate attention of a national, wise, and prudent administration, whenever we shall be so happy as to have such a one. The King of Prussia has 130 thousand good troops, ready to take the field tomorrow, but I don't find His Prussian Majesty is, at present, at all inclined to begin a war, which I am very glad of.

I observed in your Lordship's letter, *in regard to G. Grenville, an implied exclusion.* I don't mean to enter upon that point, but, that I would submit to your consideration, whether a *total* exclusion of my Lord Temple, and his brothers, and of my Lord Lyttelton, will quite answer the view and plan of settling a lasting administration, which should go on with ease and success. But this is a consideration more proper for those, who are to undertake the administration, than for myself who am only a wellwisher.

And now I mention myself, your Lordship will allow me to observe, that howmuchsoever I am pleased with the hopes of seeing such an administration as may answer the expectations of the publick and our friends, I cannot but feel the very great slight that is put on me by His Majesty and his Ministers, the Duke of Grafton and Mr. Conway. That I, after so many years of service, (I may say not unsuccessful,) to the publick, and particularly to His Majesty's royal family, repeatedly owned by His Majesty during the little time I had last the honor to be in the King's service, I, who was the first sacrificed to my Lord Chatham's boundless ambition, whose first view was to debauch and detach my nearest relations, (in which he had too much success,) and also some of my oldest and best friends, in order to make me less able to resist his power on any occasion, where it might be arbitrarily exercised ; of which His Lordship has given the fullest proofs—I say it cannot but be very cruel to me, that when His Majesty and his Minister, the Duke of Grafton, were convinced that my Lord Chatham could no longer carry on his affairs, convinced to such a degree that your Lordship, equally ill-treated with myself, should be applied to in the honorable manner that you have been, and reason given to hope that proper consideration would be had for your other friends, in these circumstances, that not the least notice should be taken of me, and when I might have expected to have had an offer, at least of being restored to the office, which was taken from me, (tho' everybody knows my resolution to accept no office;) I say not to have anything said to me, or of me, either by the King or his Minister is a usage, which I do not deserve but must feel as I do.

I assure your Lordship it shall have no effect upon my publick conduct, or in any degree lessen that intimacy, confidence, and affection which I shall always wish to preserve with your Lordship, and which *nobody* and *nothing* can ever alter but yourself.

Confidence I do expect; confidence is all I want; and therefore I am persuaded your Lordship will have the goodness to let me be informed of the several steps, that shall be taken in the progress of this great affair, to which nobody can wish more proper success than myself, and must particularly hope, that I may be acquainted with all that shall pass with the Duke of Bedford and Lord Albemarle. I send your Lordship an open letter, that you may see I don't write treason to our friend, my Lord Albemarle; which I beg you will seal and forward by your first messenger.

As your Lordship has no commands for me, (which I am glad you have not,) I shall remain here, quiet and easy, depending on your goodness, that I shall be informed of what passes.

I heard accidently that my friend, the Duke of Richmond, was sent for to town. Your Lordship mentions nothing of it, so, I suppose, nothing material has passed. I did expect that I should have heard from him, and especially at this time, when he wants me so much, for the support of all his views in Sussex, which he has so much at heart.

Mr. Conway's conduct towards me surprizes me, for I think he has been wanting in making common returns to the civilities I have endeavoured to shew him, ever since I was removed from the Privy Seal, and particularly upon the marriage of his daughter; when the Dutchess of Newcastle and I sent our congratulations to him, and Lady Aylesbury, of which they have never done us the honor to take the least notice. And, when I heard that Mr. Conway was determined to quit his employment, I went from your Lordship's house to make him a visit, gave it the turn of coming to receive his commands before I went into the country; left the card with the porter; told him that we had, before, sent our congratulations upon the marriage of his daughter; I believe your Lordship will be astonished to hear that Mr. Conway has never returned my visit, or taken any notice of me, or of my civilities to him. This is surprizing, and may proceed from the resolution, which he knows was taken at Court, to have no regard to me: but that may be carrying it too far; however I relate the fact just as it is. I am sensible I have troubled your Lordship with a very long letter. I was very desirous of laying my whole thoughts at once before you, that I might not be teazing you every day with them, and when you see them thus put together you will give the attention to them which you think proper.

I conclude your Lordship can have no thoughts of going soon into Yorkshire. If you stay any time about town, (which I hope you will,) the Dutchess of Newcastle and I hope we shall have the honor and pleasure of seeing your Lordship, and my Lady Rockingham, at Claremont.

I thank God the Dutchess is quite recovered of her late indisposition and sends her best compliments to your Lordship and Lady Rockingham, in which I sincerely join, and am, my dear Lord, etc.

HOLLES NEWCASTLE.

P.S.—I forgot to insert in its proper place, that *the King's friends* must not be protected against his administration; and some examples must be made there.

Is my Lord Gower in town? Or does your Lordship know anything of him?

This was accompanied with a private letter, as follows:

Fo. 310.   July 8, 1767.

MY DEAR LORD,— I am ashamed to have detained your Lordship's servant so long; and to have troubled you with so long a letter, but, (though I am afraid I flatter myself too much,) as there is a prospect, or at least, a possibility, that a solid system of administration may be the result of the present negotiations, tho' I have little or no concern in them, I thought in justice to your Lordship, as well as to myself, that I ought to lay my thoughts fully before you with regard to the solid interests of this country. For I know you think that places and employments should not be the sole object. For that reason I have entered largely into foreign affairs; my intelligence relating to them is certainly true. When you come to fix your administration, you will be much puzzled to find out a real proper Secretary of State. There are so few that have ever applied themselves to it, or have the least knowledge of it. *Don't* fly out.—There is no doubt but that Sandwich knows more of the matter than all of them put together; but there are objections to him, which cannot be got over. All the rest, with regard to their knowledge, (except Holdernesse,) know pretty much alike, that is, very little.

I don't know what the Duke of Grafton intends for himself. He did not seem to me, when he was there, to make any great figure in it. I really believe my Lord Hardwicke or my Lord Gower would make the best; my Lord Harwicke, who I believe would make the best, cannot, in our present system, be preferred to my Lord Gower.

Your Lordship will see that I am full of schemes; I am very sensible that I have nothing to do with them, and perhaps nobody *likes* that I should: but I am really so weary of those Bute fluctuating administrations, and so desirous of seeing such a one established as one might support with honor; and (what is the first object with me) such a one as may secure a good parliament; that I shall fling out everything that may contribute to it.

I know your Lordship talks in confidence to the Duke of Portland. Nobody has better intentions, or, in my humble opinion, better judgment. I have this moment received a very full and particular account from His Grace of what passed, last night, at the meeting at your house. And if I comprehend it right, (and it is so clear, that I think I cannot mistake it) I very much approve what passed, and particularly the very proper judgment that was made of the motives for the proposed exclusion of Mr. Grenville, and the resolution that, I understand, was taken upon it, to let *it appear* to be the King's act, and to shew a readiness to satisfy Mr. Grenville with any other employment, except the Southern Secretary of State.

Your Lordship sees I am very ready to approve the opinion of my friends, when I think it right, tho' my own opinion is neither asked nor desired; and even in that case, I am too apt to give it.

I am very impatient to hear the answer from Woburn, and the terms of my Lord Albemarle's commission. I see Mr. Conway constantly attends you. I beg pardon for giving your Lordship so much trouble and am with great truth and respect,

My dear Lord &c.

HOLLES NEWCASTLE.

Tho' no application had been made to me, or any notice or mention of me, either by the Ministers, or by my Lord Rockingham in his discourse with them, yet, as I most heartily wished success, and was desirous to support Lord Rockingham and the new administration, if founded upon the principles I liked, I thought in justice to my Lord Rockingham, and indeed to myself, that it was my duty from the long experience that I had had in business, and with a true regard for the solid interest of my country, to lay before Lord Rockingham my thoughts upon the general conduct, which an administration, founded upon national and constitutional principles, ought to hold ; and what ought to be their principal objects ; and consequently I wrote to him, from the fulness of my heart, those two material letters. I hope His Lordship, when the time comes, will shew a firm attention to them, and I am the more encouraged to hope he will, as his conduct, at present, seems entirely agreable to my ideas. In all events I have acted as an honest man, and shall have the comfort of having suggested my thoughts, which I flatter myself will stand the test of all those who know and are really concerned for the true interests of their country. But in justice to our friend, the Duke of Portland, I cannot omit a letter which I received the 8th inst. giving a very particular account of what had passed at the conference: I shall therefore give you the whole of it with my answer.

Fo. 313 b.   'Charles Street, Berkeley Square : July 8, 1767.

'DUKE OF NEWCASTLE,—MY DEAR LORD,—As the Marquess told me he had written you a long letter, last night, I imagine he sent you the particulars of the conversation that had passed between the Duke of Grafton and himself, and I therefore shall confine myself to giving an account of the sentiments, and opinions of such friends as I met there.

'I went to Grosvenor Square in the evening, and found there, the Duke of Richmond, Lords Frederick and John Cavendish, Sir Chas. Saunders, Admiral Keppel, and Mr. Burke, who, in general, seem to think that the exclusion of George Grenville and his friends is pretended, either with a view to make our union with the Duke of Bedford and his friends impracticable ; or, at least, in case the union should take effect without the Grenvilles, to leave that party open for application at any future time, when the Court might be dissatisfied with us, or have made such breaches or divisions amongst us as, I ventured to say, would be the first object and immediate attempt they would make upon our coming into power.

'Upon this ground, therefore, the Duke of Richmond, (on whom your Grace's wishes and advice have had certainly a very good and strong effect,) is of opinion, that Lord Rockingham should not begin by mentioning to the Duke of Bedford the total exclusion of the Grenvilles, but should first try how far the Bedfords are willing to embark without them; that, if upon opening his commission to treat with them, they should immediately insist upon the Treasury for Grenville, that then he should acquaint them with the negative the King has put upon that particular subject, but be ready to engage to support Mr. Grenville for any other employment, that he, or they, may wish, except the Southern Department, provided it includes America. In this idea I think both the Cavendishes concurred, and no one was warmer in it than Lord Frederick; Saunders, and Keppel gave little advice and Burke was so constantly going to and fro, that I could scarcely collect his opinion. Some time after Lord Rockingham came in with General Conway, and taking Saunders and myself apart, told us the purport of the conversation with the Duke of Grafton, in which I observed that the line of union was not sufficiently extensive, that I thought the Grenvilles ought to be included at any rate, provided they would yield the Treasury and American Department, and that whether the Duke of Bedford gave them up or not, they ought, for many reasons, to be considered. It did not appear to me that either Lord Rockingham or Saunders materially differed with me. They did not, I think, see so strongly the necessity of pushing the Grenvilles in case the Duke of Bedford should not make a point of it. But Saunders declared he should give no advice but for us to take care of our own honor.

'We then went upstairs where we talked this matter very fully over again, and pressed extremely the points I have before stated. Lord Rockingham sat down to write to Lord Albemarle, who is still at Woburn, and I came home. Thus, my Lord, I think I have given your Grace a circumstantial and I hope a not unsatisfactory account of what passed last night.

'It is impossible for me to wait upon you today nor did I ever intend it; my proposal was to have that pleasure tomorrow; but as I shall now be inclined to defer my departure for at least a day or two more, I think it may be as well to postpone my coming to Claremont 'till Friday, when we shall certainly know the result of the message to Woburn, and perhaps many other particulars which may be curious and interesting. However I submit the choice to your Grace, and leave you to decide the day of my coming to you.

'One circumstance I picked up relative to the Grenvilles, that I can't help communicating to you, tho' I must beg you not to take any notice of it, as it was told me accompanied with the like request. "Lord Thomond asked a friend of mine what was going on?" To which he answered, "You probably know more than I do; as I understand it has been communicated to Lord Gower." That is no reason, says Lord Thomond, for he is not my friend; you know my attachment is to Mr. Grenville. Well then, said my informer, what will Mr. Grenville do? Why, says Lord Thomond, whoever the offer comes to, ought to have the choice.

'How far George Grenville's inclination may be collected from this, your Grace is best able to judge. I think it is not immaterial to be known; and therefore acquaint you with it.

'I beg your Grace to present my best compliments to the Dutchess of Newcastle, who, I hope, continues to recover her health, strength, and spirits, and to believe me, with truest regard and affection,

'My dear Lord etc.
'PORTLAND.'

To the above letter I returned this answer.

Fo. 316 b.   July 8, 1767 (½-past 6).

DUKE OF PORTLAND,—MY DEAR LORD,—This whole day has been so taken up in writing volumes of advice to my Lord Rockingham, upon the short account he sent me, last night, of what passed with the Duke of Grafton, (which advice I am sure your Grace will approve, tho' I am afraid my Lord Rockingham will take but little notice of it,) that I have been obliged, 'till this moment, to defer my thanks to your Grace for the clearest, the kindest, and the most satisfactory account, that I ever received, of what passed at my Lord Rockingham's meeting, upon the overtures made by the Duke of Grafton.

Your Grace has fully supplied the defects of your friends to me. And I am now fully informed of all I want to know, the sentiments of Lord Rockingham's friends on this occasion, and I see with pleasure the great hand, that gives them, that neither Lord Rockingham nor any of his favorites will venture to give you any contradiction and that consequently everything went as your Grace and myself wish it.

Nothing could be properer or more approved by me, than the judgment formed upon the Duke of Grafton's proposal of the implied exclusion of Mr. Grenville; and the conduct proposed to be held upon it by my Lord Rockingham with the Duke of Bedford.

I beg you would let the Duke of Richmond know how much I approve his behaviour. I am not vain enough to think it is owing wholly to my advice, but His Grace has certainly acted agreably to it.

However glad we always are to see your Grace at Claremont, I entirely approve your putting off your visit 'till you can form some judgment, as to the event of this affair; particularly 'till you know the answer from Woburn and my Lord Rockingham's final resolution upon that, and upon the present negotiation

I have indeed two views in wishing your Grace would stay in town, 'till this affair is brought to some conclusion; *First* that you would be with my Lord Rockingham; I hope and think he would be directed by you. *Secondly* that I may have true and sensible accounts of all that passes both at Woburn and with the Duke of Grafton, and General Conway, who I find is now come to be the first man with my Lord Rockingham: I cannot but find myself extremely hurt that no notice has been taken of me, the first sacrifice to my Lord Chatham's boundless ambition, either by the King or his Ministers, the Duke of Grafton or Mr. Conway. *Thirdly*[1] that my Lord Rockingham does not think it necessary for him to consult me, or ask my opinion on any one step he takes in this affair.

It would not have been unworthy of His Lordship, if he had told the Duke of Grafton, that he must, in the first place, communicate everything to the Duke of Newcastle; neither would it have been too much condescension for His Lordship to have come down hither, to know my opinion, before he had had this meeting.

His great predecessor my Lord Chatham, who was then in the height of his glory and thought himself at the head of everything, vouchsafed to come to me at Claremont, to acquaint me with what had passed with the King; but as I said, your Grace supplies all those defects.

My fish post shall constantly call upon you, every day; and I am sure you will send me constant accounts by him. The Dutchess of Newcastle is, if possible, fonder of you, than I am. I thank God she is pure well and sends her kindest compliments to your Grace.   I am, &c.

After this I must add my letter to my Lord Albemarle, at Woburn; which I have mentioned in my last letter to my Lord Rockingham; and which was to go by his messenger.

[1] MS. *Secondly.*

July 8, 1767.

LORD ALBEMARLE,—MY DEAR LORD,—I received, last night, after I was in bed, from my Lord Rockingham, an account of what passed at the meeting with the Duke of Grafton, which I own in general pleased me, but that which gave me the greatest satisfaction was Lord Rockingham's proposal to communicate it to the Duke of Bedford; and the Duke of Grafton's ready consent to it, and expectation that my Lord Rockingham would make the proposal. This gives me some hopes, that we may at last see a stable, national, united administration formed; which would do the business of the nation; restore peace and quiet to the kingdom; and give respect and dignity to the King's government. And your Lordship has long known, and I hope the Duke of Bedford also, that my opinion was, and ever will be, that *that* cannot be brought about but by a thorough union between His Grace and his friends, and Lord Rockingham and his friends, of which I hope there is now a good prospect.

I shall be impatient to hear the first account from Woburn. I told my Lord Rockingham that I did not doubt but your instructions would be proper, and I am sure you would execute them with the greatest zeal and pleasure.

Any other administration that is not formed upon this united plan, must depend upon my Lord Bute for its success and *duration*. And that, I am sure, neither my Lord Rockingham nor the Duke of Bedford would consent to.

I beg you would make my most respectful compliments to the Duke and Dutchess of Bedford. The Dutchess of Newcastle, (who desires you would make her compliments also) and I hope to have the honor to see their Graces at Claremont according to their kind promise, when they come next to London.

The Dutchess of Newcastle desires her thanks to your

Lordship, for your kind concern for her. I thank God she is now compleatly recovered of her late indisposition, and we both hope that after you have happily finished your negotiation at Woburn, you will go to Buxton, and find such benefit from the waters there, that your health may be perfectly re-established in every respect, and your Lordship perfectly easy and happy.

I was very happy with the account you gave me of your supper; I was as happy with that supper, as any one that was there; but I shall be infinitely more so, at receiving a line from your Lordship, that your affairs at Woburn go to your satisfaction. Nobody can wish that more than myself, or be with more respect and affection than I am,

My dear Lord, etc.,
HOLLES NEWCASTLE.

P.S.—This goes by the Marquess's messenger. I conclude you will receive one every day, as the negotiation advances.

I am afraid you will not be able to read this letter. I have wrote two volumes to the Marquess who is but short to me.

My Lord Rockingham's letter, of the 9th, will shew, also, the extreme proper foot upon which His Lordship has put this negotiation; and my answer of the same date will shew how much I approve his conduct in this great point. This really makes me happy, as I think there is great reason to hope that a solid, constitutional, united, administration may now be formed.

Fo. 321 b.   'July 9, 1767.

'DUKE OF NEWCASTLE,—MY DEAR LORD,—Late last night I received Lord Albemarle's answer from Woburn; and as the Duke of Richmond would call upon your Grace, and give you an account this morning, I delayed writing 'till now, being indeed far from well, and being obliged to write to several of our friends (to none of whom I had wrote before, since this matter came on,) to desire them to come to London.

'I have wrote to Mr. Chas. Yorke, Lord Hardwicke, and Mr. Dowdeswell, and I shall write to Lord Dartmouth and Lord Scarborough and some others

'I have fixed Saturday for going to Woburn, and shall scarce return before Sunday morning.

'On Sunday morning I hope your Grace will come and that you will dine here. And I shall get some of our considerable friends to be here.

'Lord Albemarle's answer expressed much satisfaction at Woburn, warmth upon the subject of the removal of a certain corps; and thoughts, that to do it effectually, Mr. Grenville and his friends would be necessary: and then acquainted me that Rigby would be with me in the evening. About ten o'clock he came, in a very good humour; he said it was necessary, and incumbent upon them, to communicate with Mr. Grenville, and that he would go to Wooton today and meet me on Saturday at Woburn.

'I explained to him, that in correctness I thought, that it would not be proper that any message should go from me to Mr. Grenville. That the proposition was to us, and inclusive of the Duke of Bedford's friends; but seemed limitted there. But that in the present state it appeared very proper for the Duke of Bedford and his friends, (if thought proper,) to communicate with Mr. Grenville. And that great good might arise if, thro' the Duke of Bedford etc., any insight might be got, on what plan and how a general junction of the three parties might be made. That I thought the Duke of Bedford's weight might be a means of procuring moderation in that quarter etc. Rigby said that was what they should try, and that then they should be able to judge what they should do.

'The Treasury in my hands might be a bar to G. Grenville. But that they (i.e. the Duke of Bedford etc.) considered that point as now over, as it was offered to me.

'I was not wanting in all civilities and compliments to the

Duke of Bedford etc. I heartily wish some good may come. Saturday will give us a full insight; and then on Monday we shall have all the matter before us.

'It is unlucky for me to be very full of pain during this time of hurry and bustle. I keep myself as quiet as I can; and shall act as cooly [*sic*].

'I hope the Dutchess of Newcastle continues mending. This weather is miserable for invalids.

'I am, my dear Lord etc.

'ROCKINGHAM.'

Fo. 323 b. Claremont: July 9, 1767.

LD. ROCKINGHAM,—MY DEAR LORD,—Your letter has made me extremely happy. I approve every word in it and as a proof of it, this letter shall be very short, as I have nothing to add or to wish more, than to wish you success upon your present plan. And, I own, I do not at all despair of it.

The approbation or consent on the part of the Bedfords to your Lordship's having the Treasury is all we could wish, or desire, of them; and your Lordship's consent to their communicating what has passed to G. Grenville, and a disposition in a proper manner to satisfy them, will, I dare say, enable the Duke of Bedford to bring him to reasonable terms.

I will attend you with great pleasure on Monday morning. I approve extremely your meeting: and hope they will all come. You must send to the Duke of Richmond, or otherwise he does not propose to be in town so soon. You mention nothing of my Lord Mansfield. I hope you will see him before you go to Woburn. I am persuaded he will do right especially if the Bedfords come in roundly. He is certainly your Lordship's sincere friend, and wellwisher. The offer of the King, of the Treasury, will strike him; and, believe me, he is more necessary than anybody.

Lord Lyttelton dined here this day, in his way to the country.

He was in very good humour, seemed to know little, and you may imagine, I communicated nothing to him.

He seemed to suppose there had been offers from the court but that all was now over ; that your Lordship had insisted that Lord Albemarle should be put at the head of the army ; and that Charles Yorke should be Chancellor. I told him, so much I knew, that there was not the least truth in either of those reports.

The French ambassador has sent me word that he will dine here on Saturday. I have sent to his friend, my Lord Mansfield to meet him ; I don't believe he can come on account of his sittings. If he should, let me know what I should say to him. I wish you would see him yourself, for indeed, my dear Lord, we must carry him with us. Lord Camden would be a most insignificant man, and always depend upon my Lord Bute, and my Lord Chatham Besides the Great Seal in the hands of a true friend will give great weight in the choice of a new Parliament.

If you find the Duke of Bedford in the temper I wish and believe him to be in, I should think you might, in general, sound him upon the disposition of employments, and I should wish also to know your own thoughts, privately, when I come to town.

Possibly I may be some use to you, I assure you I will do no hurt ; I am not in that disposition.

I hope you will begin by vacating the Treasurer of the Household ; that you may give either to my Lord Edgecombe, who had it last ; Ld. Geo. Cavendish, if he would like it, and who had it ; or Lord Charles Spencer, who would certainly like it, as would the Duke of Portland, and all our old friends · I must repeat to you how happy I am in seeing the part you take in this critical conjuncture. You will get honor, credit, and reputation by it, and therefore I will only add, go on, and fear nothing.

Ever your's
HOLLES NEWCASTLE.

P.S.—The Dutchess of Newcastle sends her best compliments, in which I join, to your Lordship, and Lady Rockingham.

On the 11th inst., I had a short letter from my Lord Rockingham, enclosing one from Lord Albemarle. As they shew the happy progress of this negotiation I shall transcribe them both.

'Grosvenor Square: July 10, 1767.

'DUKE OF NEWCASTLE,—MY DEAR LORD,—I enclose to your Grace, a letter from Lord Albemarle. Tomorrow morning I set out for Woburn. Admiral Keppel goes along with me. It is needless to write on speculation, when we are so near the time of knowing, with some certainty, the material points on which we shall be to judge and act. Things look favorably and may end well; I shall be happy to send your Grace a good account.

'I am ever my dear Lord etc.

'ROCKINGHAM.

'P.S.—I hope the Dutchess of Newcastle continues mending. I am rather better but not much.'

Fo. 326 b. 'Woburn Abbey: July 10, 1767.

'DUKE OF NEWCASTLE,—MY LORD,—I was last night favored with your Grace's letter from Claremont by the Marquess' messenger; and am happy to agree so exactly with your Grace upon this negotiation with the Bedfords.

'I have had two most excellent letters from the Marquess. The Duke of Bedford is greatly satisfied and pleased with the attention towards him and his friends; and most sincerely wishes to see, (and will contribute everything in his power) a strong administration formed, such a one exactly as your Grace has pointed out in your letter, that will stand in defiance of Lord Bute and all court intrigues; such a one His Grace thinks will want the assistance of Mr. Grenville and his friends, and so do I.

'His Grace hopes, and believes, that Mr. Grenville will be reasonable, and thinks that as the Treasury has been offered to the Marquess that he can have no pretensions to it. Rigby, who is to see Grenville tomorrow, is to hold that language to him, and to endeavour to prevail upon him to support, if not to take a part in, an administration formed of the Duke of Bedford's and your Grace's friends.

'His Grace is apprehensive that if he does not join, and our demands should be thought unreasonable at court, that my Lord Bute will send to him, and that they will be able, with the support of the closet, to form a very strong, able, and formidable administration. He recommends prudence to the Marquess; and great caution not to engage himself in a hurry; has, and ever will have, his suspicions of every proposal made, as long as the Bute influence remains at court, which he thinks is stronger now if possible than ever it was.

'The Marquess is to be here on Saturday, and Rigby is to meet him from Mr. Grenville's. You shall be very exactly informed by me of everything that passes at that meeting.

'I ought to be at Buxton; I am far from well, but I shall stay here a few days longer, at the risque of my health, to promote this union, which your Grace and I so heartily wish, for the good of our country, and the mutual advantage of our friends; we can have no other views.

'I had ordered my post-horses the very day the Marquess' letter came, not dreaming of any thing of this sort, and thinking my friends upon the road to the country.

'I hope your Grace will be able to keep our friends reasonable about G. Grenville; the Duke of Bedford will not support him, if he is not so.

'The Duke and Dutchess desire their compliments to your Grace, and the Dutchess of Newcastle; I beg to add mine and to express the satisfaction I feel at Her Grace's recovery.

'The Duke of Bedford bids me tell you that he is happy to find that you and he agree so entirely; and that if we agree together and fail now, we shall be the stronger for it next winter; and must come in upon our own terms before the meeting of parliament; that the present negotiation is of that consequence, that it should be attended to with prudence and circumspection. I desired Rigby, who promised he would, to call upon you if you was in town.

'I am etc.

'ALBEMARLE.'

I shall add my letter to Lord Rockingham of the 10th as that continues the narrative, and explains what is mentioned in a former letter relating to General Conway.

Fo. 329. Claremont: July 10, 1767.

LORD ROCKINGHAM,—MY DEAR LORD,—Good journey and good success to you, with my best compliments, and wishes to the Duke and Dutchess of Bedford, and Albemarle.

I have a letter from Lord Mansfield, that he cannot come tomorrow. I hope you will see him before you go to Woburn. Your intended visit there will I am sure be a good introduction.

I am at present in high joy and expectation. I find my friend, the Duke of Portland, is stronger if possible in every thing than I am.

My friend the Duke of Richmond has acted very kindly by me with Mr. Conway. The secret is out, I was not mistaken. Mr. Conway would not be commonly civil to me, because he had heard I was strongly for G. Grenville, who was his enemy.

The Duke of Richmond told him how much he was in the wrong. I never knew there was any competition between them; the question was what was to be done when Mr. Conway was out of the Ministry, which he was looked upon to be, but enough of all that.

Our respects to Lady Rockingham.

I am etc.
HOLLES NEWCASTLE.

From all these letters you will have seen a full account of the state of this great affair to Lord Rockingham's setting out for Woburn, on Saturday the 11th inst. Immediately upon his return from thence, which was late on Sunday night, His Lordship wrote me the following short letter.

Fo. 330.

'Grosvenor Square: July 12, 1767.
'Sunday night, near 2 o'clock.

'DUKE OF NEWCASTLE,—MY DEAR LORD,—I am only this instant returned from Woburn and hope to have the honor of seeing your Grace in less than twelve hours. I can only now say that appearances are more and more favorable. The Duke of Bedford most cordial, and the result of Rigby's visit at Wooton and Stowe[1] adds much to the general promising aspect.

'I am anxious to see your Grace soon and hope you will come here when you come to town.

'Lord Albemarle's letter was wrote at Woburne, and will probably give your Grace some more circumstances.

'Upon the whole I am sure your Grace will like what has passed, but what may ensue must still remain uncertain for some time.

'I am etc.
'ROCKINGHAM.'

My Lord Rockingham also sent me a very satisfactory letter from my Lord Albemarle as follows—

[1] George Grenville's and Lord Temple's.

'Woburn Abbey: July 12, 1767.

'DUKE OF NEWCASTLE,—MY LORD,—I have the pleasure and great satisfaction of informing your Grace that our negotiation here is beyond my warmest wishes.

'Lord Temple and his brother have desired the Duke of Bedford to assure your Grace, and the Marquess that they are ready, willing, and most desirous [1] of supporting an administration with my Lord Rockingham at the head of the Treasury, upon the great plan of removing the Bute interest from court. And my Lord Temple farther declares, that if this negotiation should go off, (and he believes it will) and should he be sent to, he will give the very same answers, in the closet, that the Marquess does upon this occasion. The Duke of Bedford makes the same declaration.

'This intelligence, I am sure, will please you as much as it does me.

'I wish my health was as good as your Grace's, that I might return to town, and see this very important negotiation out; but I must go to Buxton, or I shall not be in a situation, next winter, to give my poor assistance to my friends in or out.

'The Duke and the Marquess have been very explicit to one another. I must refer you to him for particulars of their conversation; I was not present.

'The Admiral who travels with the Marquess can give you a more particular account than I can.

'I am in great spirits and am persuaded your Grace will approve of every thing. We have drank your health every day; you are very well here; and the House of Woburne desire their most sincere compliments to your Grace. I beg my respects to the Dutchess of Newcastle and am most perfectly and truly

'Your very faithful humble servant,

'ALBEMARLE.'

[1] Cf. Grenville's letter of the same date (iv. 43), and his account of the whole negotiation (pp. 48-52). Also the Duke of Bedford's account in Cavendish's *Debates*, pp. 604 *sqq.*

I communicated the whole of this very important negotiation as it stood, when my Lord Rockingham went to Woburn, to the Archbishop of Canterbury.[1] Upon which, tho' very ill with the gout, His Grace sent me the following answer, which with my letter to him I here give you.

Fo. 332. Claremont: July 10, 1767.

ARCHBP. OF CANTERBURY,—MY LORD,—The esteem and regard which I have for your Grace, the high rank in which you so deservedly are, and your goodness to me upon all occasions, make it incumbent upon me to give you the earliest notice of every thing that comes to my knowledge, that concerns the political state of this kingdom, which has too long laboured under the uncertainty, and insufficiency of annual and fluctuating administrations; if what offers at present should succeed, and be a remedy for that national inconvenience, your Grace, and every honest man, will be rejoiced at it.

I will make no other preface, but send your Grace the original accounts, which I have received; my Lord Rockingham's conduct upon them; and my thoughts and advice upon the whole. I have endeavoured to inculcate the absolute necessity of a cordial union with the Duke of Bedford, without which nothing can be solid and lasting; and thro' the Duke of Bedford's means to dispose Mr. Grenville, and his friends, to moderation and compliance. I must do justice to my Lord Rockingham, he seems to proceed with great prudence, and to desire a thorough cordial union with the Duke of Bedford etc.

Your Grace will see the liberty I have taken, in throwing out my thoughts of what ought to be the objects of a prudent, and constitutional administration, so that in all events I have done my duty, and shall have nothing to reproach myself with. Your Grace will see that I feel the slight put upon me by His Majesty, and his Ministers. That when I had been the first

---

[1] Thomas Secker.

sacrifice to my Lord Chatham's boundless ambition, and when His Majesty has thought proper to call back my Lord Rockingham, from the high station, from which he was removed, not a civil compliment, nor the least notice taken of me either by the King, or his Ministers, the Duke of Grafton and Mr. Conway. But no personal consideration shall influence my publick conduct. I shall see with the greatest pleasure such an administration established, as I hope is now in negotiation; and I shall give them all the assistance in my power, both in the forming an administration, and in the support of it afterwards.

I have ordered my servant to be at Lambeth tomorrow morning before your Grace is stirring, and he has directions to stay the whole day, or as long as your Grace may detain him, that you might have full time to read, and digest the several material letters I have the honor to send you; and to favor me with your Grace's thoughts upon them; and your advice as to myself, and the conduct you will see I have held, and propose to hold.

I beg your Grace would then send me the letters back by my servant, for I have no copies of them.

I thank God the Dutchess is perfectly recovered from a fever, and pains in her head and limbs, for which she was twice blooded. She begs me to present her respectful compliments to your Grace.

     I am with the highest respect etc.
         HOLLES NEWCASTLE.

Fo. 334 b.   ' Lambeth: July 11, 1767.

'DUKE OF NEWCASTLE,—MY LORD,—Your Grace hath honored me with a communication of which I am very unworthy at all times; and particularly unfit to make the proper acknowledgements of it at present, having the gout in my left hand and shoulder and right heel.

'But your Grace hath explained everything so distinctly in

your letters, that very little attention is necessary to understand the whole, with the reasons, and I have the happiness of agreeing with your Grace, and applauding you, on every single opinion and sentiment, which you have expressed.

'It would have been affectation to omit saying what you felt on being passed over. Yet I verily believe, shame hath been in part the cause, joined with an uncertainty, how the overtures made will end. If they produce the desired effect, there cannot fail to be declarations to your Grace, that the step taken, last year, was a wrong one, and that you act now a most honorable part in supporting such measures, as are necessary for the publick welfare. Yet, if any person, even the greatest person, should fail in this respect, go on to behave with dignity; resent nothing; and be assured that your character, your services, and your influence, will not only bear you up, but oblige others to have recourse to you.

'Lord Rockingham seems frank and cordial, and sensible of his want of your Grace's advice and assistance. I wish he may be able, by the means of it, to settle things rightly; and that the settlement may prove lasting. It may, if they please, who are concerned that it should. How long they will all, or enough of them, be so pleased, I cannot help doubting. But the rule is to try and hope for the best. To this hope, my love to my country induces me, in the first place: and in the next, my earnest wishes that the evening of your Grace's life, which hath been devoted to your country, may be as comfortable and pleasing to you, as is possible. I congratulate your Grace on the Dutchess of Newcastle's happy recovery; and beg, you will present to her the very humble respects of your Grace's most obliged and most faithful servant

'THOS. CANT.'

When Lord Rockingham returned from Woburn, I sent the Archbishop the account of His Lordship's success. His Grace's answer to my letter, on this occasion, (both of which I insert) shews his sentiments upon it.

July 13, 1767.

ARCHBP. OF CANTERBURY,—MY LORD,— Your Grace having not been displeased with the accounts I sent you, the other day, I take the liberty to enclose you a copy of a letter I received this morning from my Lord Albemarle, who was at Woburn, whilst my Lord Rockingham was there.

My Lord Rockingham was highly satisfied with his visit; (as your Grace will see by the enclosed letter that he had reason to be). If it should please God to bring this negotiation to a happy issue, this country may be in a more happy situation, than it has been for many years; and the publick interest thought of, instead of private cabals, and contests for power.

I am infinitely honored with your Grace's good opinion and approbation of my sentiments, and weak endeavours for the publick service.

I am, with great respect, etc.

HOLLES NEWCASTLE.

Fo. 336 b.   'Lambeth: July 13. 1767.

'DUKE OF NEWCASTLE,—MY LORD,—Matters go on very well thus far, but the better they go, the less likely they will be to meet with approbation in a certain place. The consequences of so strong an administration will be foreseen; and a negative will be put upon the admission of it; unless there appear to be hope of dividing it. And then all will be as bad as ever. But I rather think, a resolution will be taken to go on in the present road with some few internal changes; and to pick up additional strength by such methods, as have too often proved effectual. May these be only the low-spirited imaginations of a man in very great pain! But in all circumstances, your Grace's

' most faithful humble servant

THOS. CANT.'

On this day, Monday, the 13th inst., there was a meeting at my Lord Rockingham's, when the answer to be given, by His Lordship to the Duke of Grafton, was agreed upon, and was to the following effect.

That my Lord Rockingham, having learnt the opinion of his own friends, and also that of the Duke of Bedford, and some of His Grace's friends ; and the Duke of Bedford, having learnt also the sentiments of Lord Temple, and Mr. Grenville, my Lord Rockingham had found an equal disposition in all, to assist and support an administration for carrying on the affairs of the kingdom, with zeal, and *activity*. My Lord Rockingham desires to know whether it was His Majesty's intention, that *he* should prepare a *comprehensive* plan of administration, for His Majesty's consideration ; that if *that* was His Majesty's intention, my Lord Rockingham should desire to have the honor to attend His Majesty, to receive his *more particular* commands, upon a subject of that high importance.

The view of this was, that if there was no intention to form such an administration, as would be able to do the King's business, and that of the nation, with ability and credit, that then my Lord Rockingham would decline taking any share in it.

On Wensday, the 15th, my Lord Rockingham received this answer from the Duke of Grafton.

[It is the letter of July 15, 1767, published in the 'Bedford Correspondence,' iii. 366, 367. The Duke of Grafton conveys the King's message that Rockingham is to specify the plan on which he and his friends would come in. The Duke of Newcastle then gives Rockingham's reply of the same date, printed pp. 367, 368. Rockingham's plan would be to consider the present administration at an end. Also the Duke of Grafton's answer of July 17 (p. 378): the king is not willing to exclude any denomination of men attached to his person. If Rockingham will form a comprehensive administration in accordance with those views, the King will summon him for an interview.]

After receiving this letter from the Duke of Grafton, my Lord Rockingham despatched a messenger with a letter, to Woburn, to acquaint the Duke of Bedford with the contents of it; and to desire His Grace would come to town, to assist in settling this great point.

The Duke of Bedford returned an immediate answer, which is here subjoined with another from Lord Rockingham.

[The Duke of Bedford's letter, July 18, is in his 'Correspondence,' iii. 381, 382. He will send for Lord Temple and Mr. Grenville, and hopes to turn the 'chicane' in the construction of the word *comprehensive* against the Duke of Grafton's party. The Duke of Newcastle gives also Rockingham's answer of the same date, expressing his gratitude to the Duke of Bedford. ('Bedford Correspondence,' iii. 381.)]

My Lord Rockingham also summoned several of his friends to meet on Monday the 20th inst., which accordingly they did, in order to consult what was further to be done. But before I enter upon the account of what passed, at this meeting, I must tell you that I acquainted the Archbp. of Canterbury with the state of the negotiation, as it stood at this time, July 20th, upon which I had the following letter:

'Lambeth: July 20, 1767.

'DUKE OF NEWCASTLE,—MY LORD,—I humbly thank your Grace for the honor of your letter, and the others inclosed with it. I am sorry to say that the affair appears to me in the same light that it did a week ago, but rather more strongly. I wish the Marquess may prove the better fencer, and hope, that, if he disarms his adversary, he will do him no manner of hurt only not return his sword to him.

'I am etc.

'THOS. CANT.'

XIV

Fo. 367 (and 342).   Newcastle House July 21, 1767.

Narrative of what passed here last night.[1]

The following is, as near as I can recollect, a true account of all that passed here last night with the Duke of Richmond, Duke of Portland, Marquess of Rockingham, Admiral Keppel, Mr. Dowdeswell, Duke of Newcastle, Duke of Bedford, Earl of Sandwich, Visct. Weymouth, Mr. Rigby.

This meeting was appointed here, at the request of the Duke of Bedford, and my Lord Rockingham, and lasted till near two o'clock this morning.

It is necessary to premise, that my Lord Rockingham having desired the Duke of Bedford to come to town, His Grace came accordingly on Sunday evening, and my Lord Rockingham had two hours discourse with him on Monday morning, of which His Lordship gave me the following account, when he came from Bedford House. My Lord Rockingham was very well satisfied with the Duke of Bedford; but was extremely otherwise with some passages in the letters, which Mr. Grenville had wrote to Mr. Rigby, after Mr. Grenville had seen and known everything that had passed between my Lord Rockingham, and the Duke of Grafton.

Those passages were, to the best of my remembrance, that my Lord Rockingham, and his friends, should declare that they would *assert* and *establish* the superiority of this country, over it's colonies; that Mr. Grenville must have satisfaction as

---

[1] A full narrative of the meeting got into Almon's *Political Register* (i. 201) as 'An impartial account of a late interesting conference.' Rockingham was indignant, and wrote to Newcastle on the subject (Albemarle's *Life of Rockingham*, ii. 57). Walpole speaks of the Cavendishes who 'run about town publishing the issue of the conference.' For further accounts see *Grenville Correspondence*, iv. 76 sqq.; *Bedford Correspondence*, iii. 382-389; *Walpole* (Barker), iii. 43-65; *Burke's Correspondence*, i. 132-149.

to *men* and *measures*, and that his friends should have a becoming share of employments; but did not mention who his friends were, or what employments he expected for them. That, after the King had agreed to what should be proposed to him for Mr. Grenville's friends, he (Mr. Grenville,) would then declare his sentiments upon it.

The greatest part of the time at this meeting was taken up in debating several points, relating to the *declaration* proposed for my Lord Rockingham and his friends to make. His Lordship took it up with great warmth. He thought such a question or declaration was injurious to his honor, and declared that he would never make it, and that he would give his reasons in parliament for not doing it; as it was injurious to imagine him capable of giving up the superiority of this country over its colonies. This occasioned long debate and altercation, and much warmth from the Duke of Richmond.

The objections to the declaration proposed were, that it carried with it a very unjust suspicion, and imputation; and also, that the words *assert*, and *establish*, implied a consent to the doing something immediately, for that purpose, without any new incident, that might give occasion for it.

The Duke of Bedford endeavoured to soften and reconcile things in a most amicable and prudent manner; that he, the Duke of Bedford,) desired no such declaration; that he was perfectly satisfied himself, from the frequent conversations which he had had with my Lord Rockingham, and the rest of us, that there was no occasion for it: but Mr. Grenville had not had those opportunities; and therefore he might reasonably desire some farther satisfaction than His Grace might think necessary. And it was also to be considered, that Mr. Grenville, having been disappointed in his great object, the Treasury, and being to engage to support the Marquess of Rockingham, in that high station, which carried with it the power of Minister also, Mr. Grenville might be a little sore; and from thence possibly might fling out some expressions, which otherwise he would not have done.

That the Duke of Bedford was persuaded, that Mr. Grenville meant nothing unreasonable, or to do anything at present, if new incidents should not arise to make it necessary; and that the Duke of Bedford would declare, that he understood Mr. Grenville to mean no more by the proposed declaration; and that, if he did mean more, he, (the Duke of Bedford,) should differ from him and should tell him so very plainly.

This declaration, on the part of the Duke of Bedford, was so clear and satisfactory, that all of us were pleased with the explanation; and in order to ascertain it, Mr Dowdeswell, with His Majesty's consent, took it down in writing; to which my Lord Rockingham, and the rest of us, consented; but that which was very unfortunate was, that Mr. Rigby said,[1] *that he believed Mr. Grenville would not agree to the Duke of Bedford's explanation.*

This increased the warmth and jealousy of my Lord Rockingham and the Duke of Richmond, who infer'd from thence, that Mr. Grenville was not sincere in the declaration he had made by the Duke of Bedford, of supporting my Lord Rockingham at the Head of the Treasury; and that it was all a design to find out some pretence to depart from any engagement, or supposed promise, that he might have made to the Duke of Bedford for that purpose.[2]

The Duke of Bedford did, in the course of the night, fling

---

[1] Cf. Rigby's account of the meeting, *Grenville Correspondence*, iv. 80-83.

[2] In the margin is noted: 'The letter complained of from Mr. G. Grenville to Mr. Rigby was read; but, not having read it myself, I cannot give a very distinct account of it: but the great objection drawn from it, by my Ld. Rockingham, was, that that letter contained the whole plan of their proceedings; and was, in substance, adopted by the D. of Bedford, and Mr. Rigby; that the declaration about America; the *becoming* number of Mr. Grenville's friends to be taken care of; the satisfaction about men and measures; and lastly, the suspicion about the Duke of Grafton, and Mr. Conway, and the carrying on the negotiation thro' them, were

out, that he knew it had been often suspected that His Grace might be influenced by others to act contrary to his own opinion: but that when he had once formed an opinion, he was not very apt to change it, or to that effect. It was then understood that the Duke of Bedford should inform Mr. Grenville of His Grace's manner of understanding the declaration proposed, according to what Mr. Dowdeswell had taken down in writing: but the warmth and jealousy increased so much, on both sides, that nothing, I think, was determined about it.

The Duke of Bedford depending entirely upon Mr. Grenville's acceptation of the Duke of Bedford's interpretation of the sense of the declaration, said, *You may go on*, meaning, as was thought, to form the plan to be delivered to the King. Some general discourse was had about it; and then, I think, my Lord Rockingham said, the Duke of Grafton and Gen¹ Conway must be comprehended in the plan, as was understood, for ministerial employments.

It was very unlucky that in the course of this meeting the Duke of Richmond had dropt to Mr. Rigby, that it was proper that Mr. Conway should be comprehended, which Mr. Rigby immediately told the Duke of Bedford.

Upon which, after my Lord Rockingham had mentioned the Duke of Grafton and Mr. Conway, the Duke of Bedford, in decent but strong terms, expressed his great surprize that Mr. Conway should be thought of for a civil employment, and that he

contained in that letter, and were, as my Lord Rockingham apprehended, so far adopted by the D. of Bedford and Mr. Rigby, . . .

'That my Lord Temple and Mr. Grenville were masters of the negotiation, and for that reason, Lord Rockingham thought it was better to break it off, at that time. This is purely matter of opinion; in which I entirely differ from His Lordship. For I am persuaded, had not the unfortunate question about Mr. Conway arose, which my Lord Rockingham finds *couched* in Mr. Grenville's letter, and which, in my opinion, arose singly from my Lord Rockingham's mentioning it at last. I say it is my opinion that, had no such mention been made of Mr. Conway's remaining in administration, as civil Minister, all the other difficulties relating to Mr. Grenville and America, would have been got over by the Duke of Bedford.'

understood that *that* had been long settled, at Mr. Conway's own desire, another way; that Mr. Conway had quitted the Secretary's office, and was to return to the army. That the Duke of Bedford thought *that* a very right measure, and that he would join in carrying Mr. Conway as high in the army as he himself could wish or propose.[1]

The Duke of Richmond, very unfortunately, then said, has your Grace any objection to Mr. Conway?

The Duke of Grafton complained extremely at that question being put to him; but said, since I am forced to speak, I will. That he thought Mr. Conway a very improper civil Minister in the House of Commons, that His Grace had never approved his conduct there as such, and that he never would consent to Mr. Conway's having the conduct of the House of Commons.[2]

It was strongly insisted upon, both by my Ld. Rockingham and the Duke of Richmond.

The Duke of Bedford touched upon the Duke of Grafton, but did not finally object to his having an employment, and, I think, made some observation, that my Lord Rockingham's own position was, that *the present administration* was supposed *to be at an end*, and *a new one* to be formed: but that, upon this plan, the two material Ministers in the present administration, were in some shape, or other, to be continued. I am not certain whether the Duke of Bedford mentioned this or not at the meeting: but it is an observation that His Grace has made.

But that which the Duke of Bedford complained most of was, that after ten days intimate correspondence and negotiation with my Lord Rockingham, that after my Lord Rockingham had been down at Woburn, the Duke of Bedford had never heard one word of Mr. Conway, till that night, it came out, at

---

[1] 'For that Mr. Conway had served with great honor and reputation in the army.' Added in the margin.

[2] On his failure as a parliamentary leader, see *Lecky*, iii. 94. The favour he lent to lenient measures towards the American colonies was sufficient to make him objectionable to George Grenville.

the meeting.¹ And His Grace compared it a little, (tho' with great temper and civility,) with the treatment he had met with from my Lord Chatham, who had sent for the Duke of Bedford to town to fix the employments for the Duke of Bedford's friends; that the First Lord of the Admiralty, and the Chamberlain's office, were both then vacant by the resignation of the Duke of Portland and Sir Chas. Saunders, and when the Duke of Bedford came to meet my Lord Chatham, His Lordship told him that the King had sent for Sir Edward Hawke to town, to put him at the head of the Admiralty. I think the Duke of Bedford mentioned this at the meeting, but I am not sure; he has, I know, mentioned it in the manner here related.

The point of Mr. Conway being insisted upon absolutely by one side, and as absolutely refused by the other, this meeting broke up; and the object of it, to the great misfortune of this country, entirely at an end.

The principal parties concerned on each side, were so determined, that there was little to be said by the rest of the company. Lord Sandwich and Lord Weymouth seemed very reasonable and desirous to bring things to a happy conclusion. I could only employ my wishes and strong recommendations, which, God knows, were very sincere, as I think the interest honor, and security of this country entirely depend upon it. The meeting broke up without any mention of meeting again, very civilly, but, with mutual declarations, on both sides, that both parties were now at liberty to proceed, as they should think proper, and to take what part they should like, without being under the least obligation from any thing that had passed between them to consult, or have any regard to the sentiments, or conduct of the other party.²

[1] On the proposal about Conway 'forced on Lord Rockingham by the Cavendishes,' see *Grenville Correspondence*, iv. 89. See also Whately's letter, p. 94.

[2] In the margin is noted: 'The Duke of Newcastle is not certain whether this declaration was made at the first meeting or only at the second meeting at Newcastle House.'

The next morning, Tuesday the 21st, the Marquess of Rockingham and the Duke of Bedford were both with me. I had indeed sent to the Duke of Bedford, determined not quite to give it over, and, if I found the least inclination, to make one more trial.

The Duke of Bedford and my Lord Rockingham both acquainted me with what had passed that morning between them at Bedford House, my Lord Rockingham having gone hither, to recapitulate what had passed, that there might be no mistakes as to the facts.

I understood that they both agreed in the facts; but to my great concern had parted with the same firmness upon the great point of difference, with regard to General Conway, as before, and that they both looked upon the negotiation as absolutely at an end.

But determined, as I said, to try every thing, and to leave nothing, to reproach myself with, I observed to the Duke of Bedford that a meeting of ten people was much too large to talk upon such subjects as these, where persons of the first rank, and character, were concerned, and therefore, I would propose that His Grace, and my Lord Rockingham, should meet at my house, to see whether we might not still find out some means, of bringing this great affair to a happy conclusion. He said, he should be very happy to come, but as Mr. Rigby was the person who was to write his letters for him, he would propose that he should bring Mr. Rigby with him; and my Lord Rockingham should bring Mr. Dowdeswell. My Lord Rockingham was very ready to come, and accordingly the Duke of Bedford, and Mr. Rigby, my Lord Rockingham, and Mr. Dowdeswell, met me at my house, on Tuesday evening, but I am sorry to say this confined meeting ended just as the other did; with great civility and professions of regard on both sides.

It soon appeared that the affair of Mr. Conway was the principal point, the only obstacle that prevented this great, and most important negotiation from having the happy end which was desired, and such an administration proposed to His Majesty, as must have had the happiest consequences both for the King, and the nation ; and from the distress the present Ministers *seem now to be in* which will increase every day, I now think there would have been more probability of it's succeeding, and of being really carried into execution, than I had ever flattered myself with before.

But unhappily, it is now at an end, not by the refusal of the court, but by the difference of opinion amongst ourselves, which not only deprives this country of seeing such an immediate settlement as must have been satisfactory to all it's true friends, but what is worse destroys, and I am afraid will effectually prevent, any possibility of reviving hereafter that happy union, and connection, which I had flattered myself had been so cordially settled amongst us.

To return to the meeting ; little was said, on either side, but a very civil discussion of the great point in dispute ; my Lord Rockingham insisting that it was necessary for him to have the assistance of Mr. Conway at the head of the House of Commons ; giving an account of Mr. Conway's behaviour to him, (my Lord Rockingham) ever since my Lord Rockingham left the Treasury, and his resolution to leave this administration at the end of the session ; that Mr. Conway's behaviour in Parliament during the whole session, shew'd his good intention ; and that it was owing to Mr. Conway's behaviour in Parliament that the administration was so distressed that they were forced to make these advances to my Lord Rockingham. That my Lord Rockingham would not accept of them without including the Duke of Bedford and his friends in the manner proposed ; that after this, when my Lord Rockingham's sincerity towards the Duke of Bedford, and his friends could not be suspected, or doubted, he thought he had a right to insist upon having Mr. Conway in that state that might be of the most use to him.

The Duke of Bedford combated strongly, tho' very civilly, the merits of Mr. Conway; he disliked extremely his political notions, and his conduct towards him, and would not admit that he had that *merit* with my Lord Rockingham; for if he would have had any claim of that kind, he should have gone out in October last. That His Grace thought it reasonable that my Lord Rockingham, who was agreed to be the Minister, should have a friend of his at the head of the House of Commons; that his proper representative there was his Chancellor of the Exchequer, Mr. Dowdeswell, who was very capable of it, and would have the support of everybody, of all those who should be in possession of the best employments in the House of Commons, and of all His Grace's friends. That it was impossible that Mr Grenville, out of office, could be the person. That there was no one but Mr. Dowdeswell, whose station, and abilities, made him the proper person.

Mr. Charles Townshend was often mentioned; his abilities were confessed to be superior to anybody's, but nothing particular with regard to him was proposed on either side.

Mr. Dowdeswell spoke very handsomely, as to the business of this office; that he should be ready to take the lead in every thing relating to the finances, but, as to other State matters, he did not think himself sufficiently qualified, and therefore was very desirous of having Mr. Conway's assistance; and that *he* might have the general lead and conduct of the House of Commons.

Thus unhappily and infructuously this last trial ended, with great personal civility to each other, and with a declaration my Lord Rockingham made, (and which I was very sorry for,) that each party was from that time discharged from any engagement to each other, and at full liberty to take whatever part they pleased; to which the Duke of Bedford very readily agreed.

After the Duke of Bedford was gone, my Lord Rockingham told me, he thought he was now obliged to go to the King; and proposed to do it, as yesterday; and wished I would call at his house (as I did), that he might acquaint me, with what should pass in the closet: which he did, very kindly and I dare say very exactly, and is in substance as follows: my Lord Rockingham began by making his excuses for not having sooner attended His Majesty according to his commands, and with returning His Majesty his thanks, for the great honor the King had done him, by his most gracious offer of the Treasury.

His Majesty replied, that it was not an offer; that the Duke of Grafton might possibly understand it so, but the King did not mean it as such.[1]

I could not but observe to my Lord Rockingham, that this was the very same explanation, which my Lord Chatham had made to me, of the offer, in effect made to me, of a pension of £4,000 per annum *for life*;[2] and indeed was what my Lord Granby had reported of the Duke of Grafton's having exceeded his commission; and that I was persuaded, that His Majesty had said the same thing upon it, to my Lord Granby, that he had now done to my Lord Rockingham himself.

My Lord Rockingham recapitulated to the King,[3] every thing material, that had passed with the Duke of Grafton, and himself, and with the Duke of Bedford, relating to the Duke of Bedford, and his friends, and my Lord Temple and Mr. Grenville.

That my Lord Rockingham did understand, that, by what the Duke of Grafton said to him, it was then His Majesty's intention only to take in the *Duke of Newcastle*, himself, (my Lord Rockingham) and others of the late administration, in conjunction with some of the present Ministry; (N.B —The King made no answer to that.)

That the misfortune which had happened during the late administration, when the conduct and behaviour of several

---
[1] Cf. Albemarle's *Rockingham*, ii. 34; and *Grenville Correspondence*, iv. 88.
[2] See above, p. 99.   [3] 'to the King' added in the Duke of Newcastle's hand

persons, in the first stations, and employments, (as my Lord Rockingham hoped and believed not *altogether* with the King's approbation), had had such an ill effect, that it had made it difficult, if not impracticable, for that administration to go on in those circumstances ; that those difficulties would now, by having acquired strength, increase, and that therefore he had asked the Duke of Grafton whether he might not consult with the Duke of Bedford and his friends, and take them along with him.

The Duke of Grafton very readily consented, and told him that it was imagined *he would* and that there was *no objection to it*.

My Lord Rockingham then acquainted the King with the several particulars, which had passed with the Duke of Bedford, and Mr. Rigby, and particularly with his having refused to make any application himself to my Lord Temple, and Mr. Grenville, as not being within his commission. But as the Duke of Bedford desired it, my Lord Rockingham had no objection to His Grace's communicating what he might think proper to Lord Temple, and Mr. Grenville, and learning their sentiments upon it; my Lord Rockingham having not made the application himself, to my Lord Temple and Mr. Grenville, the King extremely approved; indeed His Majesty seemed very well pleased, with my Lord Rockingham's whole conduct.

My Lord Rockingham then acquainted the King with the difficulties which prevented his being able to form a *comprehensive plan* to be laid before His Majesty, and, I think, enter'd into the several particulars of the obstacles flung in the way, by my Lord Temple, and Mr. Grenville, who he did not believe were so sincere in their professions as he was persuaded the Duke of Bedford was.

He then acquainted the King, with the great difficulty of all, about Mr. Conway, and said that those difficulties had prevented their coming to any agreement, but that they had parted with great civility on both sides, and declared, that they were under no further engagements to each other, but were at full liberty to take whatever part they should think proper.¹

He also acquainted His Majesty, that the two last meetings were at my house. To all which, not even the last declaration of being at liberty to take any part, did His Majesty make one single word of reply, or even mention, to my Lord Rockingham, the making a plan upon his own bottom, that is, with his own friends only. His Majesty was extremely gracious, and civil, made a very gracious bow to my Lord Rockingham, and so His Lordship went out of the closet.

Upon coming out of the closet, my Lord Rockingham went, and communicated the whole to my Lord Grafton, who seemed, (as he might well,) very much surprized, and said 'Did not His Majesty order you to *form your own plan*? No my Lord, not one word like it.² Well, my Lord, what is to be done? Shall we meet your Lordship, Gen¹ Conway and I this night? No, my Lord, I see no use in our meeting, as every thing appears to be over.'

I told my Lord Rockingham that I did apprehend, that the Duke of Grafton would bring His Lordship the King's commands, to form a plan upon his own bottom. That after what had passed, particularly in the closet, where every word that was said was as it were out of the mouth of ——³ I hoped no one friend of His Lordship's did, or would, advise him to be forming a plan. My Lord Rockingham seemed to be as much of that opinion, and as much in that resolution, as I could wish him;—and nobody was more so than Mr. Dowdeswell, and my Lord Bessborough, who came in afterwards.

¹ In the margin is noted : 'My Lord Rockingham gave the King early to understand that in these circumstances it was impossible for him to be of any service to His Majesty.'
² In the margin is noted : 'That was a mistake; the King must have forgot; for to be sure that must have been his intention.' ³ ? Lord Bute

I cannot conclude this long narrative without expressing my great concern at the miscarriage of this negotiation, which, I must own, we have flung away ourselves,[1] and by his jealousies [2] and not suffering the Duke of Bedford to take his own way, who, I am persuaded, would have removed any *real* difficulties that should have remained; and if any such should hereafter have arisen, we might then, I think, with more propriety [and less danger, have broke with Mr. Grenville; and in which, I think, if well founded, the Duke of Bedford would have joined with my Ld. Rockingham [3]]. I may perhaps be too credulous but it arises from my firm opinion of the distress, which will immediately be brought upon this country by leaving things in the weak uncertain condition they are in at present, and giving perhaps to this weak administration, an opportunity to influence too much the choice of the next parliament.

I don't see any thing that can now prevent it; except, most providentially, the respective parties should at once determine to unite at all events, and that no condition should be insisted upon, on either side, that must destroy the whole.

I have fully declared my opinion, and my resolution, to have nothing to do, in forming any plan, or making any declaration relating thereto, without the Duke of Bedford, and his friends.

Fo. 354. July 27, 1767.

When I left my Lord Rockingham on Wensday last, I desired my Lord Bessborough to tell him that I wished he would immediately communicate, to the Duke of Bedford, what had passed with the King, at the audience he had had of His Majesty, and I find my Ld. Rockingham sent immediately to the Duke of Bedford, and acquainted him with it.

---

[1] Note in the margin, in Newcastle's hand: 'By my Lord Rockingham's insisting upon Mr. Conway's being the civil Minister in the House of Commons.'
[2] Relating to Mr. G. Grenville (in the margin, in Newcastle's hand).
[3] This entered in the margin, in Newcastle's hand.

The following letters from my Lord Rockingham to me of the 24th, enclosing a copy of my Lord Albemarle's to His Lordship of the 23rd, and my Lord Albemarle's letter to me, and my letter to my Lord Rockingham of the 25th, and His Lordship's answer to me of the 26th, will finish this whole transaction.

I must only make one remark upon my Lord Rockingham's last letter to me, of the 26th, that it is by no means an answer, (if thoroughly examined,) to my letter to His Lordship of the 25th. But as it is to little purpose to enter here into any altercation about it, I leave the letters, and the contents of them, to speak for themselves.

'Grosvenor Square: 24 July, 1767.

'DUKE OF NEWCASTLE,—MY DEAR LORD,—Last night, I was again desired to meet the Duke of Grafton, at Gen¹ Conway's, which I did.[1] The conversation amounted to little more than an explanation, that His Majesty meant to convey, that he had not *offered* the Treasury, (which he could not do out of delicacy to the Duke of Grafton,) but that there was no mistake in understanding it as intended.

'The Duke of Grafton then said, that he might say the Treasury was again open, that it was wished, that I, and our friends, would come in, that it was His Majesty's desire: and the Duke of Grafton wished I would open and try whether with him, and Gen¹ Conway, some plan could not be hit off, that might bring our friends into administration.

'I answered with all personal civility, that I was glad that the whole of what was said did not appear to come so *immediately* from His Majesty as to require an answer, and that therefore, I should consider it as conversation between myself, the Duke of Grafton, and Gen¹ Conway; and avoided much discussion of the matter, by saying, I did not see, in present, any great

[1] Cf. *Walpole* (Barker), iii. 64.

encouragement to come into administration: that I thought it was difficult to make the ground good.

'I have seen the Duke of Bedford since my audience of His Majesty; and informed His Grace of the material parts. He seemed in good humour, and did not find me otherwise.

'I am delighted with the receipt of Lord Albemarle's letter; I send you a copy, and also one to yourself. I hope to get out of town tomorrow evening, or sometime on Sunday.

'I am ever my dear Lord etc.

'ROCKINGHAM.'

Lord Albemarle's letter to Lord Rockingham—

'Buxton; July 23, 1767.

'LORD ROCKINGHAM,—MY DEAR LORD,—I received your express, about an hour after I had read Rigby's letter. Sir Charles,[1] and I, both agreed that the Grenvilles did not mean that the negotiation should take place, and wished it had broke off upon N. America instead of Mr. Conway, which Rigby laid great stress upon.

'Sir Charles was afraid that you had engaged yourself so deeply in this negotiation, as to be obliged to form an administration without the Bedfords. Your letter made us very easy upon that head. And though we are both very much concerned, (he less than I,) at the breaking up of this affair, we think your Lordship has acted with your usual spirit, and resolution, and finished it very much to your own credit, and reputation.

'My accounts say you was very warm at times; and that the Duke of Richmond seemed to take a considerable lead, at the meetings, particularly, in favor of Mr. Conway. I never was without my suspicions of the Grenville family, but I saw such a desire throughout *the whole* Bedford family, to unite with you, and your friends, that I depended upon their influence with the Grenvilles, to make them submit, at least for the present. I

[1] Sir Charles Saunders.

am sorry that I was mistaken, and that I have been with them dupes to strive. For Godsake, my dear Lord, don't loose sight of the Duke of Bedford. I hope you have not parted upon such bad terms, as to make your meeting again impossible, or difficult.

'George Grenville will certainly join Lord Bute, and the court have succeeded to their wish in disuniting a party, that sooner, or later, (connected,) must have drove them all from court.

'Sir Charles says, the sooner you get out of town, the better. The General, and he, join in their compliments to you. Buxton is an excellent place, I am surprizingly recovering. I dread a relapse, from politicks. I shall be happy to see you; as nobody is, or could possibly be more sincerely attached to you, than I am.

'I beg my respects to Lady Rockingham.

'Adieu, my dear Lord etc.

'ALBEMARLE.

'P.S.—I send my answer to Rigby, by your messenger, enclosed to my porter, who will convey it to him, and a line to the Duke of Newcastle.'

'Buxton: July 23, 1767.

'DUKE OF NEWCASTLE,—MY LORD,—Rigby's express, which I received an hour before the Marquess's, filled me with surprize and concern; I am sure your Grace and I feel alike on this unfortunate event; and how it was to be avoided, I cannot tell at this distance. Rigby lays the separation of the parties, to the insisting upon Mr. Conway's being Secretary of State; the Marquess, to the unreasonable proposals of the Grenvilles. I should neither have insisted upon the first, nor have given in to the last. That conduct, in all probability, would not have answered better; you might have lost Mr. Conway by it, without bringing the Grenvilles to give up their points, if they were not sincere in the affair. I never was without my suspicions of them, but depended upon their following the Duke of Bedford, who was most desirous, as well as all his family, of uniting with your Grace, and with the Marquess and his friends.

'I have begged the Marquess, if they have parted upon any terms, never to lose sight of His Grace. I have known more desperate cases recover'd, in skilful hands.

'I could not let a safe conveyance, (the Marquess's groom,) go, without communicating my poor thoughts to you.

'The waters agree surprizingly with me. I hope to wait upon your Grace and the Dutchess of Newcastle, (to whom I beg my respects,) with the Bedfords, at Claremont, before the summer is over.

'I am, with great truth and esteem, etc.

'ALBEMARLE.

'P.S.—Sir Charles desires his respects to your Grace.'

Claremont: July 25, 1767.

LORD ROCKINGHAM,—MY DEAR LORD,—I am very much obliged to your Lordship for your letter; and the communication of the letters enclosed in it. I send your Lordship a copy of the letter, which I received, by your messenger, from my Ld. Albemarle.

I am most sensibly mortified at your Lordship's intention to go to Yorkshire, without my having the honor and pleasure of seeing you, at Claremont, according to your promise,—what an appearance must it have to the world?

I have too sensibly felt, thro'out this whole negotiation, the little regard that was had to my opinion; and that I did not make my court, by telling my thoughts, as an honest man, and I am sure, as a very sincere friend, to your Lordship; when, if ever, all that has passed in this negotiation shall come to be known, I flatter myself, that those who are real friends to your Lordship and this country, will think, that, if my wishes had been followed, it might have been better *for both*.

I think I see plainly from my Lord Albemarle's letters, that I do not differ much in opinion from him, and Sir Charles Saunders.

Mr. Rigby puts the breach entirely upon the insisting upon Mr. Conway; and I cannot but agree with him. For, as to the declaration proposed by Mr. Grenville, relating to America, it was so whittled down by the Duke of Bedford, that it could not *finally* have made any difficulty. And I own it is my firm opinion, that, if you had left all this altercation with Mr. Grenville to the Duke of Bedford, His Grace (for whose sincerity in this case I will answer, as well as for my own,) would never have supported Mr. Grenville so far, as to break off the negotiation upon it. And I will still go farther; if your Lordship's and the Duke of Richmond's suspicions of Mr. Grenville should have proved true, and Mr. Grenville should act a false part, you might better have parted with him, when that should have happened, than have broke off the negotiation now, upon this account. But to be sure, as Mr. Rigby says, the insisting upon General Conway's remaining the Minister in the House of Commons, was, and is, the great point. When I heard of it by hance some days ago, and told your Lordship of it, it indeed surprized me as much as it did the Duke of Bedford. I took the liberty then to tell your Lordship, I believed the Duke of Bedford would not agree to it. And also that I knew, and I do know now, that some of your Lordship's best friends would not approve of it. I have all the honor imaginable for Gen[l] Conway: but his anger with me goes all to the same point, and shews his rooted aversion to those, who are now against his remaining a civil Minister.

I must beg leave to put your Lordship in mind of one circumstance, relating to Mr. Conway, which I could wish he thought of at this present time. It happened at my Lord Northington's, when the Duke of Grafton, and Mr. Conway, were insisting upon the necessity, for the sake and salvation of this country, that Mr. Pitt should come in, upon *his own terms*; and that, when one of his terms was the declaration he made to my nephew, Mr. Thos. Townshend, Junr., *that he* (Mr. Pitt,) *would not sit at Council with the Duke of Newcastle*,[1] (a pretty harsh expression); and when it was known, and admitted, that Mr. Pitt intended to remove my Lord Rockingham from the Head of the Treasury;—Mr. Conway made this remarkable declaration *to your Lordship and myself*, that he thought, the salvation of that country depended so much upon Mr. Pitt's coming into the administration, that he thought both your Lordship, and I, should give way, or yield to whatever was necessary for that purpose.

Your Lordship must remember my remarkable answer to Mr. Conway, 'Sir, mine is not a common case; it is not removing me from my employment, that is nothing, but my honor must be hurt with the reason given for it; *that Mr. Pitt would not sit at council with the Duke of Newcastle*; that carries an insinuation, that I was not to be trusted, but to be considered as one not fit to be employed, from the worst cause that could be assigned.'

Did Mr. Conway retain these thoughts with regard to his country, and the duty of every man who really wished it well, to submit to anything, for the sake of it, Mr. Conway would surely be the last man to suffer this negotiation, (I mean an union between the parties concerned, which will appear to all the world to be so essential for the honor, dignity, peace, and quiet of the nation) to be broke off, *singly* because he did not remain in that civil capacity, which he himself had long declared he would not do; and, when every facility offered, for returning to his old profession in the army, which is, and was, his favorite object,) with the highest honor, and regard.

The great thing, my Lord, that hurt me the most, was the

---

[1] See above, p. 55.

strong declaration your Lordship made to the Duke of Bedford, and His Grace's assent to it, that each party were at full liberty to take what part they pleased, without consulting or considering what the sentiments of the other party might be ; and that your Lordship should acquaint the King with your having done so. Upon which, I did think His Majesty would have founded some new offer, or have given some orders to your Lordship, about a plan of administration.

I have now a complaint of a different kind to make to your Lordship: that when you know how much I have at heart, the taking the Bedfords with you in any future negotiation, that you would not let me have the satisfaction to know from yourself the proper resolution, which you seem to have taken and communicated to the Duke of Portland ; that you should not mind these proposals and declarations from the Duke of Grafton ; and that if the King thought proper to send to you, that you would desire leave, immediately, to talk to the Duke of Bedford ; and, I think, that you would not undertake anything, without the Duke of Bedford's concurrence ; and also, that you had desired your good friend the Duke of Richmond to let Mr. Conway know this ; and that you must in any case, or at your audience upon this occasion, make it an absolute condition, to consult the Duke of Bedford.

This, my dear Lord, is all you can do at present. But why would not you let me have the satisfaction of knowing it from yourself? And that, as a farther proof of your intention, you think, the Duke of Bedford was in very good humour ; and that you had parted very good friends?

I also find that you was satisfied with your discourse with Rigby, at Arthur's.[1] I think it is plain, by Rigby's letter to my Lord Albemarle, and by what Lady Weymouth said to the Duke of Portland, that the Duke of Bedford, and all his friends

---

[1] Arthur's Club.

are ready to come in with our friends, when once the great point of Mr. Conway is over. I was glad your Lordship asked the Duke of Portland's opinion upon that point before your young friends; I have known His Grace's opinion upon it, a great while; and I hope he said enough to shew your Lordship, what his real opinion was.

I conclude you have seen my Lord M[ansfield], and Charles Yorke; I could wish to have heard from you something of them. I don't doubt but I shall have a general account, at least, of what passed, from them both.

And now, my dear Lord, I have given your Lordship my opinion of the conduct, which, I could have wished, had been held; I have most sincerely lamented the breaking off the negotiation, upon the single point of Mr. Conway; in which I see the Duke of Portland, Lord Albemarle, Sir Chas. Saunders, and I believe Lord Bessborough, entirely agree with me. And this opinion is not only founded upon what I think is right, and necessary for *the publick*, but full as much so for *yourself*.

I have also expressed my satisfaction, with what, the Duke of Portland tells me, is your Lordship's resolution, in case you should be sent for to the King; and that you should always keep the union with the Bedfords in your thoughts. I pray God, you may, *in a way to bring it to bear!* Upon that plan, I shall rejoice to hear from you; and if any thing, that can tend towards it happens, let me know it from yourself.

I now most heartily wish you a good journey, and all happiness, honor, and success in Yorkshire; and that I may have the pleasure of hearing from you, when you have an opportunity which must often happen. The Dutchess of Newcastle joins with me, in our best compliments and wishes to your Lordship, and Lady Rockingham.

Ever yours
HOLLES NEWCASTLE.

'Grosvenor Square: July 26, 1767.

'DUKE OF NEWCASTLE,—MY DEAR LORD,—When I saw your Grace at Parsons Green, I then told your Grace I would pay you a visit, at Claremont, before I left London to go into Yorkshire, if the negotiation should end; and when your Grace was here, on Wensday last, you left me, in appearance, in very good humour; and I should have thought, that after all the hurry and bustle I have gone thro', and that a journey to Claremont now was, and could be, only a matter of parade, I did not think your Grace would have been so much out of humour about it.

'What speculations the world is to form upon my not going to Claremont, will be difficult to guess. I think, as it was well known, that it was *I*, who desired the Duke of Bedford and his friends, to have the meeting on Monday night, *at Newcastle House* (tho' the Duke of Bedford proffer'd to come to Grosvenor Square,) that the second meeting was again at Newcastle House, and, that the two days your Grace was in town, you honor'd me with your company, at dinner, both days; I must say also, with every other circumstance, which has happened; I hardly can conceive, that anyone could doubt of the mutual and reciprocal friendship, which subsisted between your Grace, and myself.

'Your Grace's last letter, you must allow me to say, is much too captious. You arraign me for sins of *commission* and *omission*. A general blame is thrown, that, after all the fullest proofs of Lord Temple's and Geo. Grenville's cavillings and chicaneries, and intentions to obstruct; and after we had seen at the meetings, that Mr. Grenville's and Lord Temple's letters were made the briefs, on which the whole discussions turned; your Grace seems to think it would have been better to have gone on, in hopes, that in some point or other, the Duke of Bedford and his friends might have broke off with them.

'Indeed, my Lord, I am more and more satisfied in thinking this matter over, that, according to the influence which Geo.

Grenville and Lord Temple had, in the present moment, it was much the best, to break off *now* ; and there is every appearance, that the Duke of Bedford, and many of his friends are not *now* in bad humour.

'Of the temper etc. of the Duke of Bedford and his friends, I did inform you : but omitted telling you what had happened on Thursday night, in regard to the suggestion, conveyed thro' the Duke of Richmond to Mr. Conway, for his and the Duke of Grafton's information ; and which I had not, nor have not heard, went any furthur. If your Grace could conceive, that I could have a pleasure in concealing from you that information, which might be satisfactory to you, at least I must beg of you to make this remark, that my *secret* and *concealed* transactions, in matter and intention, agree with your wishes and sentiments.

'Your Grace also seems offended, that I relinquished the Duke of Bedford and his friends, from their obliging declarations, personally to myself, on the subject of the Treasury, in regard to *future* proceedings ; and also, that I relinquished and set Lord Temple, and Geo. Grenville, *free* from their declarations, in regard to comprehensive plan. I did this on Tuesday night ; because my intentions were fixed, in regard to coming into administration, never proposing to do otherwise than I did, on Wensday ; or, what I still more confirmed, by what I did, on Thursday.

'I saw no use in tying up Lord Temple and Geo. Grenville, or the Duke of Bedford and his friends, on either of their declarations ; and I acted a handsome and more becoming part by first insisting on my own being free, and then acting as I have done. I would beg to know what use it would be to our friends, to have kept up the bargain.

'Your Grace will recollect the old story of a Governor abroad, who had not the power of punishing with death ; but he contrived to torment those whom he would have wished to have hanged, 'till he made them to hang themselves. An offer of the Treasury to me, if a negotiation ensues, with Lord Temple and Geo. Grenville, and the Duke of Bedford, and his friends, should have thought it incumbent in honor to have made to me, must have been a parallel case. Or, if Lord Temple, and Geo. Grenville should have a negotiation, and should propose that our friends should join on the comprehensive plan, I believe that too will not be wide of a parallel case. I am very clear in opinion, that it is right to keep up a good understanding with the Duke of Bedford, and his friends, but I do not think that it is at all necessary to be too *courting*.

'The suggestion to Gen¹ Conway was not quite to the degree that your Grace's letter conveys. It was, that I should have power to treat with any persons, particularly the Duke of Bedford and his friends; that I should see His Majesty in the first outset; and that, if His Majesty would honor me with his confidence, and give me ground to form an idea with more certainty, of what His Majesty would, and would not do;—if I thought the outline would do, upon full authority being given me, I would engage, and if we could not settle, either with the Duke of Bedford and his friends, or with any additional strength, I should think myself, nevertheless, bound to undertake. If this was to happen, we should be fully justified in whatever we did.

'I have seen Lord Mansfield and Mr. Chas. Yorke. I think the former in good humour; your Grace may probably hear from him or see him, and I would rather refer you to himself: but in general can say I found him cordial and friendly; and that I know, he did handsomely in a conversation he had had with the Duke of Bedford.

'Charles Yorke was with me yesterday; and intends to see you. He touched upon the subject of George Grenville, and had some thoughts and ideas arising upon that, which I told him (as far, and as well, as I could guess,) *would never do*, but upon the whole, I liked his conversation very well; and feel very easy and happy in that interview.

I have a chance of getting away tonight; but all my private business, and the winding up of all these political matters; the long accounts I am forced to send; and friends constantly calling in, hurries me exceedingly, and much adds to my earnest wishes to have a little recess.

'I shall now conclude with heartily wishing your Grace, and the Dutchess good health; and assuring you that whether in or out of humour, I shall not easily be otherwise than with truth and sincerity

'Your Grace's most obedt. and most humble servant,

'ROCKINGHAM.'

As I understand Lord Rockingham proposed to set out for Yorkshire on this day, and as the Duke of Richmond is gone to Sussex, I conclude this whole affair is ended for the present, both with the Duke of Bedford and his friends, and with the Duke of Grafton and Gen¹ Conway.

What steps the present administration may take, in their present circumstances, may be hard to guess. It is said, that they have sent for my Lord Northington, to come to town for his advice, and it is generally thought, that the Duke of Grafton will form some plan of his own; and that Mr. Conway will continue Secretary of State: but all these are mere conjectures.

If my Lord Rockingham keeps up his good humour and good disposition towards the Duke of Bedford and his friends; and if His Grace and his friends do the same, as I am persuaded they will, time and difficulties which must occur in forming any other administration, may possibly, once more, bring this negotiation on again; and in that case I pray God, it may end better than this has done.

I have heard from *a very good hand* who said *he was sure of it*, that the resolution is now taken to dissolve the parliament, after the next prorogation, to have the elections in October next; and the new parliament to meet after Christmas. I own

I could hardly believe it, but I was told it so confidently, that I cannot avoid taking notice of it; and wishing that all our friends may be prepared for such an event.

XV

Fo. 386.   Claremont : October 13, 1767.

MY DEAR OLD FRIEND,—I must own, I was never so much hurt, mortified and disappointed in my whole life, as I was, last night, by the receipt of your short, cold, and I must say, unfriendly letter of the 10th, to the warmest, most confidential, and, I think, the most interesting letter, I ever wrote in my life; wherein I pointed out to you my distress; I implored your advice and assistance; I called upon all my Whig friends, for their's; I complained most justly of the Duke of Portland's most extraordinary and amazing silence, for such a long time, even beyond the bounds of civility, in not vouchsafing to send me a common answer to my letters upon his own affairs; to all this you say not one word.—The Duke of Portland is at Carlisle; (as I knew, from my Lord Rockingham, and not from His Grace;) and that, in the middle of next month, you will lay before me the state of Retford.

I think, I hope, I see the only cause of this coolness; for I can call God to witness, that, during my whole life, ever since I had any thing to do in Nottinghamshire (which is now ever since the year 1711), my whole study has been to show my love, affection, respect, and confidence to your good father and yourself without any drawback, for one moment, in my whole life. To you I apply for advice; it is from you I expect the first assistance: but I will take it up higher. I did, and do expect, that the Whig gentlemen should, in this instance of insult from my own family, make my cause their own. I expect it from the Duke of Portland in the first instance, from the many proofs I have given of my attachment to His Grace, and his

interest, preferably even, I may say, to my own. I expect it
most particularly from His Grace, from his justice and known
regard to those who deserve it from him. For it is to my
partiality, (thought at least so) for the Duke of Portland, that
has brought all these difficulties; it is to that, I owe all this
cruel behaviour in my Lord Lincoln. Would I have made my
Lord Lincoln Lord Lieutenant, and thrown all Nottingham
into him, which he very truly thought I did not do purely out
of regard to the Duke of Portland, and our friends, my Lord
Lincoln would not have set up Col. Clinton at Newark, nor
have supported Jack Shelley [1] in this situation.

Do you wonder, I should say, *my resolution is taken*? I
have said so all along. True it is, that neither the Duke of
Portland, nor yourself, have ever made me a direct answer; but
my intention is not new to you. But now *my scold* is over,
occasioned by a disappointment I did not expect; I have done;
let us look forward.

I think the treatment I now meet with from my own family,
and the present administration, is such as ought to be resented
by every Whig in Nottinghamshire. Was your good father, my
first friend; my good friends, old Sir Fras. Molyneux, old
Thornaugh, Jos. Mellish, Plumptre, Sir G. Savile, and all those
Whigs, who lived in those days, to see a possibility of my being
drove out of Nottinghamshire, (which will, and must be, the
case) by two such ungrateful nephews, who neither now, nor
ever hereafter, could have had any thing to do in Nottinghamshire, had it not been for my means;—what would they, who
knew that it was myself, and I may almost say, myself alone,
who rescued the county of Nottingham, and all the boroughs in
it, out of the hands of the Tories; [2] the county from Willoughby

---

[1] M.P. for East Retford.

[2] For an analysis of the Duke's power in controlling elections see *English Historical Review*, No. 47, p. 448, 'The Duke of Newcastle and the Election of 1734,' by Basil Williams.

and Levinz; the town of Retford from Levinz and Digby; the town of Newark, from Willoughby; the town of Nottingham from Warren, and Sedley; —I say, what would they say, to see me, upon the point of being drove out of the county, by two such ungrateful young men; it is upon that point, that I think the Whig gentlemen should, and I hope will, take it up. It is upon that point, that I wrote the enclosed letter [1] to the Marquess of Rockingham; and I hope that will be an excuse for the warmth of this letter.

If you knew what I feel from the usage of some of my friends, you would not wonder at my warmth upon every occasion, which can bring it to my mind. To have courted Fred. Montagu in the manner I have done; to have shew'd my inclination to favor his great object, of coming in for Cambridge; [2] to have secured it for him in case of a vacancy; to have promised in all events, to secure him a seat in Parliament; to have heard not one word from him in the whole course of this interesting summer; and then to be told by his, and my best friend, *shortly, Mr. Montagu is safe for the next election.* By whose means is he safe? I aver by my means.

Nothing mortifies me so much as your taking no notice of the Duke of Portland's most surprizing silence. Does he mean to drop me; and to withdraw from that entire confidence and union in measures, which he has so constantly observed *to this time*; that is, 'till this silence began?

Does he disapprove of the contents of my letter to Lord Rockingham, upon the necessity of a thorough, unreserved union with the Duke of Bedford and his friends; that letter wrote entirely agreable to every sentiment that I thought I knew to be then His Grace's? Has he altered his opinion? or have his uncles, the Cavendishes, induced him to do it? God forbid that he should not alter any opinion, which he should think wrong; but why did His Grace not trust his best friend,

---

[1] An allusion to the Appendix.   [2] He did not do so.

from whom he never kept any thing secret before, the Duke of Newcastle, with it? The Duke of Portland, and you, can, with four lines make me easy upon all these points ; but silence or passing them slightly over, will never do it.

I once intended to send this letter by the post ; but upon consideration, and as I always designed to send a messenger to you, upon our Nottinghamshire affairs, with such other letters as I should think necessary to write, and particularly to my two agents, your friend Mr. Mason, and my old man *Jack Bristowe*, whose good wishes for me and my interest, I can depend upon, tho' not upon his discretion, I have determined to send this letter, by that messenger.

INDEX

ABDY, Sir Anthony, 97-98
Albemarle, George (Keppel), Earl of, 2-4, 9-13, 19, 47, 59, 70-71, 86, 97-99, 105-112, 116, 119, 120, 124-134, 138, 154-157, 160-161
Almon, John, 98
Argyll, John (Campbell), Duke of, 74

BAKER, Sir William, M.P., 37
Barré, Col., 96
Barrington, William Wildman (Barrington-Shute), Viscount, 6
Baynton, Sir Griffith, 41
Beckford, William, M.P., 58
Bedford, John (Russell), Duke of, 3, 7-11, 17, 21-22, 27, 42, 76, 99, 102, 106, 109, 112, 116, 120-128, 168
Bessborough, William (Ponsonby), Earl of, 29, 34, 47, 97, 109, 152-153, 161
Boroughbridge, 35
Bourbon, House of, 13
Bristowe, John, 169
Burke, Edmund, 97, 120-121
Burton, —, 97
Bute, John (Stuart), Earl of, 5-14, 17, 27-31, 42, 47, 51, 61, 64-65, 75, 80, 104, 112, 125, 129, 131, 156

CAMDEN, Charles (Pratt), Baron, 46, 52, 90, 94, 104, 110, 112, 129, and *see* Pratt
Canterbury, Archbishop of. *See* Secker
Cavendish, Lord Frederick, 29, 109, 120-121

Cavendish, Lord George, 29, 109, 120-121, 129
Cavendish, Lord John, 15, 29, 43, 46-47, 60, 86, 100, 105, 109, 120-121
Chatham, William (Pitt), Earl of, 97-99, 103-105, 112, 114-115, 124, 129, 136, 146, 150, 159, and *see* Pitt
Chavigny, Théodore de, 74
Choiseul, Etienne François, Duc de, 114
Clinton, Col., 167
Clumber, 35
Colebrooke, Sir George, 54
Conway, Henry Seymour, General, 25, 28-30, 41-47, 54-87, 94-95, 103-107, 110, 115-117, 121, 124, 132, 136, 144-165
Cooke, George, 96
Cotes, Humphrey, 98
Cumberland, William Augustus, Prince, Duke of, 2-31, 38, 54, 63, 65
Cumberland, Frederick Henry, Prince, Duke of, 70

DARTMOUTH, William (Legge), Earl of, 30, 47, 78, 96-97
Denbigh, Basil (Feilding), Earl of, 50
Despencer, Francis (Dashwood), Lord, 28, 30, 47
Digby, —, 168
Dowdeswell, William, 15, 30, 69, 80, 93, 96-97, 100-101, 105, 108, 141, 143, 147, 149, 152
Dyson, Jeremiah, M.P., 72-75, 102-104

EDGCUMBE. *See* Mount-Edgcumbe
Eglintoun, Alexander (Montgomerie), Earl of, 72
Egmont, John (Perceval), Earl of, 15-16, 23, 30, 39 42, 47-49, 58-64, 68-70, 81, 97
Elliot, —, 64
Elliot, Sir George, 104
Ellis, Wellbore, 76

FETHERSTONE, Sir Matthew, 86

GAGE, William Hall (Gage), Viscount, 97
Gloucester, William Henry, Prince, Duke of, 70
Glover, Ric., M.P., 98
Gower, Granville (Leveson-Gower), Earl, 105-106, 108, 117-118
Grafton, Augustus Henry (FitzRoy), Duke of, 21-26, 29-30, 36-49, 53-60, 71, 81, 84-85, 88, 102-112, 115, 118, 123-125, 136, 139, 144, 150-154, 160, 163-165
Granby, John (Manners), styled Marquess of, 17-20, 74, 104, 107
Grantham, Thomas (Robinson), Baron, 34, 46, 67, 86, 97
Granville, John (Carteret), Earl, 75
Grenville, George, 3, 7, 10-11, 14-20, 27, 42, 51, 76, 100, 106, 109-110, 115, 119-123, 127-164
Grenville, James, 96
Gross, M., 72, 75

HALIFAX, George (Montague), Earl of, 8, 19
Hardwicke, Philip (Yorke), Earl of, 34
Hardwicke, Philip (Yorke), Earl of, 30, 60, 65-66, 77, 81, 98
Hawke, Sir Edward, 146
Hayes, 9-15
Hewett, John, M.P., 39, 81, 99
Hillsborough, Wills (Hill), Earl of, 97
Holderness, Robert (Darcy), Earl of, 118
Holland, Stephen (Fox), Baron, 17-19, 42
Honeywood, General, 73-74
Huntingdon, Francis (Hastings), Earl of, 30

Hume, John, Bishop of Oxford, 91-92, 95
Hurdis, Thomas, 113

KEPPEL, Augustus, Admiral, 23, 71, 86, 97, 120, 141
Kingston-upon-Hull, Evelyn (Pierrepont), Duke of, 35

LEVINZ, William, 168
Lichfield, George Henry (Lee), Earl of, 28-30, 64
Ligonier, John Louis (Ligonier), Earl, 18
Lincoln, Henry (Clinton), Earl of, 35, 82, 92-93, 167
Lowth, Robert, Bishop of St. David's, 91
Lyttelton, George (Lyttelton), Baron, 7, 15, 19, 53, 115, 128

MACKENZIE, James Stuart, 17-18, 25, 28, 30, 34, 61-63, 84, 104
Manners, Lord Robert, 74
Mansfield, William (Murray), Lord, 52-53, 100-107, 112-113, 128, 130, 161, 164
Marlborough, George (Spencer), Duke of, 23, 30, 33
Mason, —, 169
Mellish, Jos., 167
Mellish, William, 37
Meredith, Sir William, 97
Molyneux, Sir Francis, 167
Montagu, Fred., 168
Montrath, Lady, 85
Moreton, John, M.P., 8
Moss, Charles, Dr., Bishop of St. David's, 91
Mount-Edgcumbe, George (Edgcumbe), Baron of, 129
Murray, Lieut.-Gen., 76

NEWCASTLE, Duchess of, 39, 91, 95, 99, 108, 116-117, 122, 124-125
Newcastle-under-Lyne, Thomas (Pelham-Holles), Duke of, 6-12, 23, 30, 54, 67-68, 71, 86, 124, 141, 150
North, Frederick North), styled Lord, 6, 69, 96

Northington, Robert (Henley), Earl of, 8, 16, 30, 40-49, 58-62, 76-79, 82, 84, 87, 90, 105-106, 113, 158
Northumberland, Hugh (Smithson), Earl of, 3-14, 29, 35, 62, 63, 84
Norton, Sir Fletcher, 28, 30, 62
Nuthall, Thomas, 54

ONSLOW, George, 70, 86, 104
Oswald, —, 96
Oxford, Bishop of. *See* Hume

PELHAM, Thomas, 15, 96
Pitt, William, 6, 9-16, 20-28, 32, 39, 43-46, 50, 53-59, 67, 71, 75-93, and *see* Chatham
Plumptre, John, 167
Portland, William Henry (Cavendish), Duke of, 7, 9, 29-30, 35, 43, 46-47, 77, 81-82, 86-87, 97-99, 105, 108-109, 119-124, 129, 141, 146, 150-151, 166-169
Potts, —, 65, 81
Powell, Dr. William Samuel, 95-96
Pratt, Lord Chief Justice, 23, 28, and *see* Camden
Prussia, Frederick II., King of, 12, 114
Pulteney, William, 75
Pulteney, General, 70

RICHMOND, Charles (Lennox), Duke of, 35, 60, 66-78, 82-90, 99, 103, 106, 116, 120-126, 132, 141-145, 155-165
Rigby, Richard, 108, 131-133, 141-147, 155-160
Rochford, William Henry (Nassau de Zulestein), Earl of, 76
Rockingham, Lady, 117, &c.
Rockingham, Charles (Watson-Wentworth), Marquess of, 6, 9-12, 21, 25-30, 36-49, 51-56, 59-71, 73-88, 97-98, 104, 108-168

SACKVILLE, Lord George, 39, 41, 96
St. David's, Bishop of. *See* Lowth and Moss
Salisbury, Bishop of. *See* Thomas
Sandwich, John (Montagu), Earl of, 19, 53

Saunders, Sir Charles, 23, 86, 97, 120-121, 146, 155-156, 161
Savile, Sir George, 23, 41, 81, 86, 99, 167
Secker, Thomas, Archbishop of Canterbury, 30, 52, 135-140
Sedley, Sir Charles, 168
Shelburne, William (Petty), Earl of, 90, 98
Shelley, John, M.P., 167
Spencer, John (Spencer), Earl, 86
Spencer, Lord Charles, 129
Stanley, Hans, 69
Staremberg, Count, 74
Stowe, 90, &c.
Strange, James (Stanley), styled Lord, 51

TALBOT, William (Talbot), Earl, 30, 50, 64, 71, 104
Temple, Richard (Grenville), Lord, 6, 9-15, 19-24, 27, 32, 42, 44, 53, 82-88, 98, 115, 134, 162-164
Thomas, John, Bishop of Salisbury, 90
Thomond, Percy (Wyndham-O'Brien), Earl of, 122
Thornaugh, John, 167
Townshend, Charles, 6, 15, 17, 25, 28-29, 65, 93, 100, 103, 149
Townshend, Charles, called Spanish, 86
Townshend, Thomas, Junior, 54-55, 159
Townshend, George (Townshend), Lord, 25
Triple Alliance, 23

VILLIERS, George Bussy (Villiers), styled Viscount, 15, 86

WALES, Princess Dowager of, 4, 5, 7-8, 71, 81
Walpole, Sir Robert, 74, 114
Walpole, Thomas, 54
Warren, —, 168
West, James, 37, 93, 100
West, Col., 70
Weymouth, Thomas (Thynne), Viscount, 103, 106, 141, 146
Weymouth, Lady, 160

White, John, M.P., *passim*
Wilkes, John, 29
Wilkinson, Thomas, 35
Willes, Edward, 98
Willoughby, —, 167-168
Wilmot, Sir John Eardley, Judge, 98, 101
Winchilsea, Daniel (Finch), Earl of, 25, 30, 47, 58-62, 105, 108-109

Wolterton, 99
Wyndham, Sir William, 75

York, Edward Augustus, Duke of, 70, 81
Yorke, Charles, 28, 30, 46, 59-60, 66, 78, 98, 106-107, 113, 129, 161, 164
Yorke, John, 97, 98

PRINTED BY
SPOTTISWOODE AND CO., NEW-STREET SQUARE
LONDON